2024 UK Air Fryer Cookbook for Beginners

1800 Days Healthy and Hot Air Fryer Meals for Your Whole Family and Busy People on a Budget

Sandra G. Green

Copyright© 2023 By Sandra G. Green
All Rights Reserved

This book is copyright protected. It is only for personal use. You cannot amend, distribute, sell, use, quote or paraphrase any part of the content within this book, without the consent of the author or publisher. Under no circumstances will any blame or legal responsibility be held against the publisher, or author, for any damages, reparation, or monetary loss due to the information contained within this book, either directly or indirectly.

Disclaimer Notice:

Please note the information contained within this document is for educational and entertainment purposes only. All effort has been executed to present accurate, up to date, reliable, complete information. No warranties of any kind are declared or implied. Readers acknowledge that the author is not engaged in the rendering of legal, financial, medical or professional advice. The content within this book has been derived from various sources. Please consult a licensed professional before attempting any techniques outlined in this book. By reading this document, the reader agrees that under no circumstances is the author responsible for any losses, direct or indirect, that are incurred as a result of the use of the information contained within this document, including, but not limited to, errors, omissions, or inaccuracies.

Contents

Amazon Air Fryer Cookbook: A Culinary Journey of Global Family Favourites 1

Chapter 1 Breakfast 6
Spicy Avocado & Egg Toasties 6
Air Fryer Berry Pancake Puffs 6
Mediterranean Chickpea Omelette 6
Air Fried Coconut & Mango Sticky Rice Bites (Thailand-inspired) 7
Crispy Air Fried Halloumi & Za'atar Toast (Middle Eastern-inspired) 7
Savory Air Fried Mochi with Seaweed & Soy (Japanese-inspired) 7
Air Fried Plantain & Black Bean Tostadas (Latin American-inspired) 8
Air Fried Peach & Almond Breakfast Pastries (European-inspired) 8
Air Fried Spinach & Feta Samosas (Indian-inspired with a twist) 9
Air Fried Rye & Salmon Bites (Scandinavian-inspired) 9
Air Fried Chorizo & Potato Empanadas (Spanish-inspired) 9
Air Fried Matcha & White Chocolate Muffins (Asian-inspired) 10
Air Fried Peri-Peri Chicken Breakfast Wraps (African-inspired) 10
Air Fried Apricot & Pistachio Granola Bars (Middle Eastern-inspired) 11
Air Fried Corn & Zucchini Fritters (Australian-inspired) 11
Air Fried Potato & Sauerkraut Pierogi (Eastern European-inspired) 11
Air Fried Banana & Nutella Spring Rolls (Southeast Asian-inspired with a twist) 12
Air Fried Stuffed Tomato & Tuna Peppers (Mediterranean-inspired) 12
Air Fried Chorizo & Egg Breakfast Pockets (Mexican-inspired) 13
Air Fried Lamb & Mint Breakfast Sausages (British-inspired) 13
Pancakes... 13
Air Fryer Banana Pancakes.. 14

Chapter 2 Lunch 15
Air Fryer Italian Margherita Flatbread 15
Air Fryer French Croque Monsieur 15
Air Fryer Chinese Vegetable Spring Rolls 15
Air Fryer Greek Spanakorizo (Spinach Rice).. 16
Air Fryer Indian Aloo Tikki (Potato Patties) 16
Air Fryer American BBQ Chicken Sliders 16
Air Fryer Moroccan Vegetable Tagine 16
Air Fryer Turkish Gözleme (Stuffed Flatbread) 17
Air Fryer Japanese Teriyaki Salmon Bowl 17
Air Fryer Brazilian Pão de Queijo (Cheese Bread) 17
Air Fryer Kenyan Samosas 18
Air Fryer Spanish Tortilla (Potato Omelette) 18
Air Fryer Vietnamese Bánh Mì Sandwich 18
Air Fryer Lebanese Falafel Wrap 19
Air Fryer Thai Basil Chicken 19
Grilled Chicken Fajitas 19
Spinach and Feta Stuffed Chicken 20

Chapter 3 Diner.. 21
Air Fryer French Coq au Vin 21
Air Fryer Indian Butter Chicken.. 21
Air Fryer Moroccan Lamb Tagine 21
Air Fryer Chinese Kung Pao Chicken 22
Air Fryer Mexican Chili Con Carne 22
Air Fryer Japanese Teriyaki Salmon 22

Air Fryer Brazilian Picanha Steak 23
Air Fryer Greek Moussaka 23
Air Fryer Kenyan Sukuma Wiki 23
Air Fryer Turkish Kofta Kebabs 23
Air Fryer Peruvian Lomo Saltado 24
Air Fryer German Bratwurst with Sauerkraut 24
Air Fryer Ghanaian Kelewele (Spicy Fried Plantains) 24
Air Fryer Italian Eggplant Parmesan 25
Air Fryer Thai Basil Chicken 25
Air Fryer Russian Beef Stroganoff 25
Air Fryer Filipino Chicken Adobo 26
Air Fryer Spanish Patatas Bravas 26
Air Fryer Korean Bulgogi 26
Air Fryer Hungarian Goulash 27
Air Fryer Moroccan Lamb Tagine 27
Air Fryer Indian Butter Chicken 27
Air Fryer British Shepherd's Pie 28
Air Fryer Vietnamese Lemongrass Chicken 28
Air Fryer Jamaican Jerk Chicken 28
Steak Diane 29
Fish and Chips.. 29

Chapter 4 Beef, Pork and lamb 30
Air Fryer Argentinian Beef Empanadas 30
Air Fryer Korean Pork Bulgogi 30
Air Fryer Moroccan Lamb Tagine 30
Air Fryer Texas BBQ Beef Ribs 31
Air Fryer German Pork Schnitzel 31
Air Fryer Filipino Beef Adobo 31
Air Fryer Italian Pork Saltimbocca 31
Air Fryer Middle Eastern Lamb Kofta 32
Air Fryer Thai Beef Satay 32
Air Fryer Hungarian Pork Goulash... 32
Air Fryer Brazilian Beef Picanha 33
Air Fryer Lebanese Lamb Kebabs 33
Air Fryer Japanese Pork Tonkatsu 33
Air Fryer Persian Lamb Koobideh 33
Air Fryer Spanish Pork Pinchos Morunos 34
Air Fryer Indian Lamb Seekh Kebabs 34
Air Fryer Greek Beef Souvlaki 34
Air Fryer Mexican Pork Carnitas 34
Air Fryer Australian Lamb Chops 35
Air Fryer Korean Beef Bulgogi 35
French Beef Bourguignon Meatballs 35
Crispy Pork Schnitzel 36
Mexican Adobo Pork Belly Tacos with Pickled Red Onion 36
Chinese Five Spice Pork Tenderloin 37

Chapter 5 Fish and seafood 38
Air-Fried Herb-Crusted Salmon 38
Spicy Prawn Tacos with Mango Salsa 38
Coconut-Crusted Tilapia with Pineapple Chutney 38
Crispy Calamari Rings with Aioli Dip 39
Lemon-Herb Haddock with Asparagus 39
Spiced Mussels with Tomato Sauce 39
Thai-Inspired Fish Cakes with Sweet Chili Sauce 40
Moroccan Spiced Shrimp with Couscous 40

Brazilian Coconut Fish Stew (Moqueca) 40
Japanese Teriyaki Glazed Eel (Unagi) 41
Greek Octopus with Lemon and Oregano 41
Vietnamese Lemongrass Clams 41
Peruvian Ceviche Tostadas 42
Swedish Dill and Lemon Butter Shrimp 42
Indian Tandoori Lobster Tails 42
Peruvian Ceviche Tostadas 43
Swedish Dill and Lemon Butter Shrimp 43
Indian Tandoori Lobster Tails 43
Italian Seafood Risotto Arancini 44
Filipino Garlic Pepper Squid 44
Cajun Shrimp and Grits 44
Cajun Blackened Salmon 45

Chapter 6 Vegetable and Vegetarian 46

Air Fryer Italian Vegan Eggplant Parmesan 46
Air Fryer Middle Eastern Falafel Bowl 46
Air Fryer Indian Vegetable Samosas 46
Air Fryer Thai Vegan Pineapple Fried Rice 47
Air Fryer Mexican Vegan Stuffed Peppers 47
Air Fryer Moroccan Vegan Tagine 47
Air Fryer Japanese Vegan Tempura Vegetables 48
Air Fryer French Ratatouille 48
Air Fryer Mexican Vegan Tofu Tacos 48
Air Fryer Indonesian Vegan Gado-Gado 49
Air Fryer African Vegan Bobotie 49
Air Fryer Caribbean Vegan Jackfruit "Pulled Pork" 49
Air Fryer Spanish Vegan Paella 50
Air Fryer Mediterranean Vegan Stuffed Tomatoes 50
Air Fryer British Vegan Shepherd's Pie 50
Air Fryer Greek Vegan Moussaka 51
Air Fryer Peruvian Vegan Quinoa Stuffed Peppers 51
Air Fryer Vietnamese Vegan Spring Rolls 51
Air Fryer Middle Eastern Vegan Falafel Wraps 52
Air Fryer Italian Vegan Eggplant Parmesan 52
Indian Spiced Okra 52
Cauliflower "Steak" 53

Chapter 7 Sides and appetisers 54

Air Fryer Greek Vegan Spanakopita Bites 54
Air Fryer Korean Vegan Kimchi Pancakes 54
Air Fryer Brazilian Vegan Cheese Bites (Pão de Queijo) 54
Air Fryer Moroccan Vegan Lentil Fritters 54
Air Fryer Spanish Vegan Patatas Bravas 55
Air Fryer Chinese Vegan Spring Onion Pancakes 55
Air Fryer Italian Vegan Artichoke Bruschetta 55
Air Fryer Thai Vegan Sweet Potato Balls 56
Air Fryer Japanese Vegan Tempura Vegetables 56
Air Fryer Russian Vegan Stuffed Mushrooms 56
Air Fryer African Vegan Plantain Chips 56
Air Fryer Mexican Vegan Elote Bites 57
Air Fryer British Vegan "Fish" and Chips 57
Air Fryer Middle Eastern Vegan Spinach Fatayer 57
Air Fryer Italian Vegan Stuffed Olives 57
Bacon-Wrapped Jalapeño Poppers 58
Fried Pickles 58

Chapter 8 Soups and Stews 59
Air Fryer Tomato Basil Soup 59
Air Fryer Moroccan Lentil Stew.. 59
Air Fryer Creamy Mushroom Soup 59
Air Fryer Spicy Thai Coconut Soup (Tom Kha Gai) 60
Air Fryer Hungarian Beef Goulash 60
Air Fryer Spanish Gazpacho 60
Air Fryer Russian Borscht 60
Air Fryer Japanese Miso Soup with Tofu 61
Air Fryer French Onion Soup 61
Air Fryer Brazilian Black Bean Soup (Feijoada) 61
Air Fryer Irish Potato Leek Soup 62
Air Fryer Mexican Tortilla Soup... 62
Air Fryer Italian Minestrone Soup 62
Air Fryer African Peanut Stew 63
Air Fryer Thai Coconut Soup (Tom Kha Gai) 63

Chapter 9 Snacks 64
Air Fryer Brazilian Coxinhas (Chicken Croquettes) 64
Air Fryer Italian Arancini (Rice Balls) 64
Air Fryer Korean Tteokbokki (Spicy Rice Cakes) 64
Air Fryer Indian Samosas 64
Air Fryer Greek Spanakopita (Spinach Pie) 65
Air Fryer Moroccan Lamb Kefta Meatballs 65
Air Fryer Australian Vegemite and Cheese Scrolls.. 65
Air Fryer Mexican Taquitos 65
Air Fryer Thai Sweet Potato Balls 66
Air Fryer British Scotch Eggs... 66
Air Fryer German Pretzel Bites 66
Air Fryer Jamaican Jerk Chicken Wings 67
Air Fryer Vietnamese Spring Rolls 67
Air Fryer Russian Pirozhki (Stuffed Buns) 67
Air Fryer Kenyan Bhajia (Potato Fritters) 67
Meatballs with Hot Dipping Sauce 68
Mini Apple Pies 68

Chapter 10 Chapter Desserts 69
Air Fryer Italian Cannoli... 69
Air Fryer French Madeleines 69
Air Fryer Japanese Mochi 69
Air Fryer American Brownie Bites.. 70
Air Fryer Indian Gulab Jamun 70
Air Fryer British Scones 70
Air Fryer Moroccan Coconut Ghriba 70
Air Fryer Australian Lamingtons 71
Air Fryer Russian Sharlotka (Apple Cake)... 71
Air Fryer Chinese Red Bean Buns 71
Air Fryer Filipino Turon (Banana Spring Rolls)... 72
Air Fryer Dutch Poffertjes (Mini Pancakes) 72
Air Fryer Greek Loukoumades (Honey Balls) 72
Air Fryer Brazilian Brigadeiros (Chocolate Truffles) 72
Air Fryer South African Malva Pudding.. 73
Chocolate Lava Cakes.. 73
Bread Pudding with Caramel Sauce 74

Amazon Air Fryer Cookbook: A Culinary Journey of Global Family Favourites

Introduction to the Culinary Revolution:

In every epoch of human history, there have been groundbreaking advancements that have reshaped the way we live. Introducing the air fryer in culinary arts stands out as a modern marvel.

This device is not just another kitchen gadget; it's a revolutionary tool that promises to redefine cooking. Think about the countless hours spent in front of the stove, the litres of oil used, and the waiting time before ovens reach the desired temperature.

The air fryer simplifies this, making cooking quicker, healthier, and more efficient.

1. What is an Air Fryer?

The air fryer, a revolutionary kitchen appliance, has transformed how we perceive frying. At its core, an air fryer is a countertop convection oven that circulates superheated air around food. Unlike traditional frying methods that submerge foods in oil, an air fryer uses minimal oil, harnessing the power of circulating hot air to cook foods to crispy perfection. The result? Food that boasts the beloved crispy layer of traditional frying but with a fraction of the fat and calories.

2. 20 Tips and Tricks for Using an Air Fryer:

- Preheat: Just like an oven, preheating your air fryer can result in more consistent cooking.
- Avoid Overcrowding: Allow room for hot air to circulate freely.
- Shake the Basket: Shaking ensures even cooking, especially for foods like fries or vegetables.
- Use Minimal Oil: A light spritz or brush is often enough.
- Layering is Key: Use parchment paper if you're layering food to prevent sticking.
- Watch for Smoke: If the air fryer smokes, it's a sign there's too much oil.
- Keep it Clean: Regular cleaning prevents unwanted smoke and flavours.
- Use Accessories: Special pans or racks can expand your cooking options.
- Avoid Aerosol Sprays: They can damage the non-stick coating.
- Tweak Traditional Recipes: Traditional oven recipes can be adapted by reducing the cooking time by 20% and lowering the temperature by about 25°F.
- Add Water: For fatty foods, adding water to the drawer can prevent smoke.
- Check Foods Early: Due to its efficiency, foods can be done sooner than expected.
- Safety First: Use oven mitts or tongs, and avoid touching the interior during or immediately after use.
- Breading Matters: For a crispier finish, consider double breading.
- Mind the Size: Cut foods in similar sizes for even cooking.
- Temperature Matters: Adjusting the temperature can help achieve the desired crispness.
- Use the Right Oil: Opt for oils with higher smoke points, like avocado or grapeseed oil.
- Rest Your Food: Let your food sit for a few minutes after cooking for the best texture.

- Stay Nearby: Due to its quick cooking, it's best to stay close to prevent overcooking.
- Experiment: The air fryer is versatile. Try various recipes and find your favourites!

3. Embrace Healthy Eating with Your Air Fryer:

The air fryer isn't just a kitchen gadget; it's a pathway to healthier eating. Drastically reducing the need for oil minimises the intake of unnecessary fats and calories. Foods retain most nutrients, as they aren't lost in a vat of oil. From crispy vegetables to juicy meats, the air fryer ensures you get the best of both worlds: delightful taste and nutritional value. Moreover, with a reduced risk of harmful compounds like acrylamide, you can enjoy fried foods without typical health concerns. In an era where health and well-being are paramount, the air fryer is a testament to innovation that caters to our taste buds and overall health. Embracing the air fryer means embracing a harmonious lifestyle where flavour and health coexist.

A Global Gastronomic Tour:

Food is more than just sustenance; it's an experience. It holds stories of ancient civilisations, tales of voyages, and chronicles of innovation. Every bite tells a story of a place and time, making dining a journey.

This cookbook is designed to take you on a global culinary expedition. Every recipe is a passport to a new destination, from the bustling streets of Mumbai to the tranquil beaches of the Mediterranean, from the historic Silk Road to the modern metropolises of the Americas.

Rediscovering the Joy of Cooking with the Air Fryer:

The air fryer is not just about convenience; it's about rediscovering the joy of cooking.

Remember the first time you baked a cake or made your first stew? The anticipation, the excitement, the joy of sharing your creation with loved ones.

The air fryer brings back that joy, making cooking less of a chore and more of a delightful experience. Whether you're whipping up a quick snack or preparing a feast for a special occasion, the air fryer ensures that your dishes are cooked to perfection every time.

A Mosaic of Global Dishes:

Our world is a vibrant mosaic of cultures, traditions, and flavours. Every corner of our planet, from the bustling markets of Asia to the serene countryside of Europe, teems with culinary treasures waiting to be discovered. This cookbook mirrors that diversity, presenting dishes that range from age-old traditional recipes to contemporary culinary wonders. The rich tapestry of global cuisines is woven into these pages, offering a taste of history, tradition, and innovation. As you flip through the pages, you'll find recipes that have travelled through time, carrying stories, secrets, and the soul of the places they come from. Some dishes have been passed down through generations, preserving the legacy of ancient civilisations, while others are inspired by modern culinary trends, showcasing the ever-evolving nature of global cuisine. Be it a dish from the old Silk Road, reminiscent of traders and explorers, or a modern fusion creation that marries contrasting flavours in harmony, and each recipe offers a unique culinary adventure. Through these dishes, we are savouring flavours

and embarking on a journey that bridges continents, cultures, and epochs.

Benefits Beyond Convenience:

The health benefits of using an air fryer cannot be emphasised enough. We often reach for the quickest, most convenient meal options in today's fast-paced world. However, speed and ease don't have to come at the expense of our health, and the air fryer is a testament to that. As society becomes more health-conscious, there's a growing demand for cooking methods that are not only convenient but also healthy. Enter the air fryer, a revolutionary appliance changing how we perceive "fast food."

The air fryer delivers on both fronts: speed and health. Using superheated air to cook food eliminates the need for excessive oil. This drastically reduces calorie and fat intake, allowing for a healthier alternative to traditional frying methods. But the benefits don't stop there. Harmful compounds sometimes produced during conventional frying, like acrylamide, are significantly reduced with an air fryer.

Moreover, the air fryer is versatile. Its range is impressive, from crispy fries to tender chicken and baked goods. This means dietary restrictions or preferences, such as gluten-free or vegetarian diets, can easily be catered to. It opens up culinary possibilities while ensuring you're eating clean and healthy.

Another notable benefit is the preservation of nutrients. Foods cooked in an air fryer tend to retain more vitamins and minerals because they're exposed to heat for a shorter duration. This is especially beneficial for vegetables, ensuring they maintain their nutritional integrity while achieving a palatable texture.

The economic benefits are worth noting too. Using less oil means spending less money over time. Additionally, since air fryers cook faster than conventional ovens, you'll save on electricity bills in the long run.

Furthermore, the safety aspect of air fryers is commendable. The closed cooking system reduces the risk of oil splatter, which can cause burns or accidents in the kitchen. Plus, most models come with auto-shutoff features, minimising the risk of overcooking or potential fire hazards.

The air fryer is not just a kitchen appliance; it's a lifestyle change. It promotes healthier eating habits, encourages culinary experimentation, and aligns with the modern ethos of living well. You're not just investing in a product; you're investing in your health, well-being, and peace of mind. In a world where we're constantly juggling time, health, and responsibilities, the air fryer emerges as a beacon of balance, proving that convenience and health can go hand in hand.

Health Benefits of Air Fryers:

The air fryer is more than just a modern kitchen gadget; it's a boon for the health-conscious. Its innovative cooking technique ensures that dishes retain maximum nutrients while preserving the authentic flavours and textures we love. By significantly reducing the need for oil, it reduces harmful trans fats and cholesterol. This primarily benefits those aiming for better heart health, weight management, and overall well-being.

Regular deep frying can lead to excessive calorie and fat intake, but with an air fryer, you can achieve the same crispy results without immersing food in oil. This not only helps in reducing calorie intake but also promotes healthier cholesterol levels. Moreover, air fryers reduce the risk of harmful compounds like acrylamide, which can form in certain foods during high-heat cooking methods like frying. Acrylamide has been linked to potential health risks; reducing its presence a noteworthy benefit of air frying.

Additionally, the consistent and even circulation of hot air in an air fryer ensures that food is cooked uniformly. This means fewer chances of undercooked sections, thus reducing potential risks associated with consuming certain undercooked foods. The faster cooking times also mean that nutrients, especially the heat-sensitive ones, have less time to break down, leading to nutritionally more decadent meals.

With an air fryer, you're not just indulging in delicious food but also making a conscious choice for a healthier lifestyle. It's an investment in your health, allowing you to enjoy your favourite dishes with minimal guilt. As more individuals become aware of their dietary choices and their impacts on health, the air fryer stands out as a versatile tool that aligns with the principles of healthful eating without compromising taste.

A Universal Language:

Food, in its essence, is so much more than just sustenance for the body. It is the one language that transcends borders, cultures, and generations. It's a universal medium of expression, a tool for storytelling, a means of preserving history, and an art form passed down through millennia. Every bite we take carries a narrative, a memory, a sentiment, and a legacy. From the spices traded on ancient Silk Roads to the modern fusion dishes inspired by global migration, food charts the journey of civilisations, communities, and individuals.

This cookbook pays homage to this universal language, presenting recipes that tell stories of love, adventure, struggle, and triumph. Each dish is a window into a different world, a different time, and a different life. They reflect the heartbeats of grandmothers who passed down family secrets, the innovations of chefs who dared to think outside the box, the resilience of communities that adapted and thrived, and the love of parents trying to introduce their heritage to their children.

Through these dishes, we don't just relish flavours; we embark on journeys. We travel across meandering rivers, through bustling markets, into humble kitchens, and around grand banquet tables. We meet people from all walks of life, from the farmer who takes pride in his produce to the child tasting her first ice cream. We experience celebrations, rituals, and everyday moments that, while seemingly mundane, form the fabric of our shared human experience.

Moreover, food has the incredible power to evoke memories and emotions. A single aroma can transport us back to childhood, a forgotten moment, or a cherished loved one. It bridges gaps, starts conversations, and fosters understanding. In a world that often feels fragmented, food reminds us of our commonalities, the bonds that unite us, and the flavours that remind us of home, wherever that may be.

Every page in this cookbook is an invitation to explore, learn, and connect. It's a testament to food's power to unite, heal, and celebrate life. So, as you delve into these recipes, remember that you're not just preparing a meal; you're partaking in a rich tapestry of stories, traditions, and emotions that span the globe and echo through time.

From the Novice to the Maestro:

Cooking is an art, a skill, and a passion that evolves with time and experience. Like a painter's brush or a musician's instrument, the kitchen becomes a canvas for both the novice and the maestro. This cookbook is crafted with this in mind, ensuring that every culinary enthusiast, irrespective of their proficiency, finds value, guidance, and inspiration within its pages.

For beginners, it's natural to feel daunted when faced with unfamiliar techniques, exotic ingredients, or intricate recipes. But remember, every seasoned chef once stood where you are, pondering where to start. This cookbook serves as a stepping stone, introducing you to the basics while offering the comfort of clear, concise directions. It instils confidence, encouraging you to experiment, adapt, and enjoy the creation process.

For the culinary maestros who have mastered the dance of flavours and techniques, this cookbook offers a refreshing array of dishes to add to your repertoire. It challenges you to push boundaries, innovate, and rediscover the joy of cooking something new. Each recipe is a testament to the rich tapestry of global cuisine, presenting an opportunity to dive deeper into lesser-known culinary traditions, techniques, and flavours.

Moreover, embedded within the pages are invaluable tips, tricks, and insights gathered from seasoned chefs and grandmothers alike. They serve as pearls of wisdom, ensuring that each dish you create resonates with authenticity and love. These knowledge nuggets elevate your culinary creations, be it the secret to a fluffier dough, the perfect temperature for a succulent roast, or the ideal sauce consistency.

In essence, this cookbook is more than just a collection of recipes. It's a journey that celebrates the joy of cooking, the stories behind each dish, and the shared experiences around the dining table. Whether you're whipping up a quick weekday meal, indulging in a weekend culinary project, or preparing a feast for a special occasion, these recipes are tailored to suit every mood, moment, and milestone.

As you embark on this gastronomic adventure, let this cookbook guide you through flavours, techniques, and memories. Here's to the joy of cooking, the thrill of discovery, and the dishes that will soon become your signature.

Conclusion:

In the end, cooking is about love. It's about expressing love for oneself, the ingredients, the environment, and those we share our food with. It's a timeless dance of flavours and aromas, a sensory experience transcending borders and periods. Every dish you prepare is not just a meal; it's an emotion, a story, a piece of art. This cookbook is a labour of love, a tribute to the world's rich culinary heritage, and a celebration of the joy of cooking. Through its pages, you'll learn techniques, recipes, and the soul and essence behind each dish.

As you turn the pages, you'll embark on a journey of discovery, experimentation, and creation, rediscovering age-old traditions and pioneering new culinary trails. You become a storyteller with every ingredient you choose and every flavour you meld, weaving tales of culture, history, and personal experiences. Each recipe invites you to explore, taste, and celebrate the vast culinary world. Cooking is also about connection, bridging the gap between generations, cultures, and continents. It's a way of preserving our history while paving the way for future culinary innovations.

Here's to many delightful meals, shared stories, cherished memories, and the countless adventures that await in your culinary journey. Embrace the beauty of cooking, for it is a language that speaks to the heart, feeds the soul, and brings us all closer together. In this shared communion of food, we find joy, warmth, and a sense of belonging.

Chapter 1 Breakfast

Spicy Avocado & Egg Toasties

Prep time: 10 minutes   Cooking Time: 8 minutes   Servings: 2

Ingredients:
- 4 slices of whole grain bread
- 1 tsp red chilli flakes
- 2 ripe avocados, mashed
- 30 ml olive oil
- 2 large eggs
- Salt and pepper to taste

Instructions:
1. Preheat the Ninja Air Fryer to 180°C.
2. Brush both sides of the bread slices with olive oil.
3. Place the bread in the air fryer and cook for 4 minutes until crispy.
4. Meanwhile, soft boil the eggs for 6 minutes in boiling water, then peel.
5. Spread mashed avocado on each toast slice. Place a soft-boiled egg on two of the slices and sprinkle with chilli flakes, salt, and pepper.
6. Sandwich with the remaining slices.

Air Fryer Berry Pancake Puffs

Prep time: 15 minutes   Cooking Time: 12 minutes   Servings: 4

Ingredients:
- 150 grams all-purpose flour
- 2 large eggs
- 50 grams sugar
- 1 tsp vanilla extract
- 240 ml milk
- 1 tsp baking powder
- 100 grams mixed berries (blueberries, raspberries, strawberries)
- Maple syrup, for serving

Instructions:
1. In a bowl, mix flour, sugar, baking powder, milk, eggs, and vanilla until smooth.
2. Gently fold in the mixed berries.
3. Preheat the Ninja Air Fryer to 180°C.
4. Using a spoon, drop dollops of the batter into the air fryer. Ensure they don't touch.
5. Cook for 12 minutes or until golden brown.
6. Serve warm with a drizzle of maple syrup.

Mediterranean Chickpea Omelette

Prep time: 10 minutes   Cooking Time: 10 minutes   Servings: 2

Ingredients:
- 100 grams chickpea flour
- 50 grams sun-dried tomatoes, chopped
- 1 tsp dried oregano
- 240 ml water
- 2 tbsp fresh parsley, chopped
- Salt and pepper to taste
- 30 ml olive oil

Instructions:
1. In a bowl, whisk together chickpea flour, water, parsley, oregano, salt, and pepper until smooth.

2. Stir in the sun-dried tomatoes.
3. Preheat the Ninja Air Fryer to 180°C.
4. Pour the mixture into a greased, air fryer-safe dish.
5. Cook in the air fryer for 10 minutes or until set and slightly golden.
6. Slice and serve warm.

Air Fried Coconut & Mango Sticky Rice Bites (Thailand-inspired)

Prep time: 20 minutes Cooking Time: 15 minutes Servings: 4

Ingredients:
- 150 grams glutinous rice, soaked overnight
- 50 grams sugar
- Toasted sesame seeds, for garnish
- 100 ml coconut milk
- 1 ripe mango, diced

Instructions:
1. Drain the soaked rice and steam until tender.
2. In a saucepan, heat the coconut milk and sugar until the sugar dissolves.
3. Mix the cooked rice with the coconut milk mixture.
4. Preheat the Ninja Air Fryer to 180°C.
5. Form small bite-sized balls of the rice mixture, placing a mango piece in the center of each.
6. Air fry for 15 minutes or until slightly crispy on the outside.
7. Garnish with toasted sesame seeds.

Crispy Air Fried Halloumi & Za'atar Toast (Middle Eastern-inspired)

Prep time: 10 minutes Cooking Time: 8 minutes Servings: 2

Ingredients:
- 4 slices of sourdough bread
- 2 tbsp za'atar spice blend
- 200 grams halloumi cheese, sliced
- 30 ml olive oil

Instructions:
1. Brush both sides of the bread slices with olive oil and sprinkle with za'atar.
2. Preheat the Ninja Air Fryer to 180°C.
3. Place the bread and halloumi slices in the air fryer.
4. Cook for 8 minutes, flipping the halloumi halfway through, until the bread is crispy and the halloumi is golden.
5. Serve the halloumi on the za'atar toast.

Savory Air Fried Mochi with Seaweed & Soy (Japanese-inspired)

Prep time: 20 minutes (excluding mochi preparation) Cooking Time: 10 minutes Servings: 4

Ingredients:
- 8 pieces of plain mochi
- Soy sauce for dipping
- 4 sheets of nori (seaweed), cut into strips
- Toasted sesame seeds for garnish

Instructions:
1. Preheat the Ninja Air Fryer to 180°C.
2. Place the mochi pieces in the air fryer.
3. Cook for 10 minutes or until the mochi puffs up and becomes crispy on the outside.
4. Wrap each mochi with a strip of nori.
5. Serve with soy sauce for dipping and garnish with toasted sesame seeds.

Air Fried Plantain & Black Bean Tostadas (Latin American-inspired)

Prep time: 15 minutes   Cooking Time: 12 minutes   Servings: 4

Ingredients:
- 2 ripe plantains, sliced
- 4 small tortillas
- Fresh cilantro, chopped
- Salt and pepper to taste
- 200 grams black beans, mashed
- 50 grams queso fresco, crumbled
- 30 ml olive oil

Instructions:
1. Brush the tortillas with olive oil on both sides.
2. Preheat the Ninja Air Fryer to 180°C.
3. Place the tortillas and plantain slices in the air fryer.
4. Cook for 12 minutes, flipping the plantains halfway through, until the tortillas are crispy and the plantains are caramelized.
5. Spread the mashed black beans on the tortillas, top with plantain slices, queso fresco, and cilantro.
6. Season with salt and pepper.

Air Fried Peach & Almond Breakfast Pastries (European-inspired)

Prep time: 20 minutes   Cooking Time: 15 minutes   Servings: 4

Ingredients:
- 1 sheet puff pastry, cut into 4 squares
- 50 grams almond paste
- Almond slivers for garnish
- 2 ripe peaches, sliced
- Powdered sugar for dusting

Instructions:
1. Roll out each puff pastry square slightly and place a dollop of almond paste in the center.
2. Arrange peach slices over the almond paste.
3. Preheat the Ninja Air Fryer to 180°C.
4. Place the pastries in the air fryer and cook for 15 minutes or until golden brown and puffed.
5. Remove and let cool slightly.
6. Dust with powdered sugar and garnish with almond slivers.

Air Fried Spinach & Feta Samosas (Indian-inspired with a twist)

Prep time: 25 minutes   Cooking Time: 15 minutes   Servings: 4

Ingredients:
- 8 samosa wrappers
- 100 grams feta cheese, crumbled
- 2 cloves garlic, minced
- Salt and pepper to taste
- 200 grams spinach, chopped
- 1 small onion, finely chopped
- 1 tsp cumin seeds
- 30 ml olive oil

Instructions:
1. In a pan, heat a tablespoon of olive oil and sauté the onions until translucent.
2. Add garlic, cumin seeds, and spinach. Cook until the spinach is wilted.
3. Remove from heat and let cool slightly. Mix in the crumbled feta cheese. Season with salt and pepper.
4. Fill each samosa wrapper with the spinach and feta mixture and fold into a triangle.
5. Brush the samosas with olive oil.
6. Preheat the Ninja Air Fryer to 180°C.
7. Place the samosas in the air fryer and cook for 15 minutes or until crispy and golden.

Air Fried Rye & Salmon Bites (Scandinavian-inspired)

Prep time: 15 minutes   Cooking Time: 10 minutes   Servings: 4

Ingredients:
- 8 small slices of rye bread
- 100 grams cream cheese
- 1 lemon, zest and juice
- 30 ml olive oil
- 200 grams smoked salmon
- Fresh dill, chopped
- Capers for garnish

Instructions:
1. Mix cream cheese with lemon zest, juice, and a handful of chopped dill.
2. Brush rye bread slices with olive oil.
3. Preheat the Ninja Air Fryer to 180°C.
4. Place the rye bread slices in the air fryer and cook for 10 minutes or until crispy.
5. Spread the cream cheese mixture on each slice, top with smoked salmon, and garnish with capers and more dill.

Air Fried Chorizo & Potato Empanadas (Spanish-inspired)

Prep time: 30 minutes   Cooking Time: 15 minutes   Servings: 4

Ingredients:
- 8 empanada wrappers
- 2 medium potatoes, boiled and mashed
- 2 cloves garlic, minced
- Salt and pepper to taste
- 200 grams chorizo, diced
- 1 small onion, finely chopped
- 1 tsp smoked paprika
- 30 ml olive oil

Instructions:
1. In a pan, heat a tablespoon of olive oil and sauté onions until translucent.
2. Add garlic, chorizo, smoked paprika, and cook until chorizo is slightly crispy.
3. Mix in the mashed potatoes. Season with salt and pepper.
4. Fill each empanada wrapper with the chorizo and potato mixture and seal the edges.
5. Brush the empanadas with olive oil.
6. Preheat the Ninja Air Fryer to 180°C.
7. Place the empanadas in the air fryer and cook for 15 minutes or until golden brown.

Air Fried Matcha & White Chocolate Muffins (Asian-inspired)

Prep time: 20 minutes   Cooking Time: 15 minutes   Servings: 4

Ingredients:
- 150 grams all-purpose flour
- 50 grams white chocolate chips
- 1 tsp baking powder
- 1 large egg
- A pinch of salt
- 2 tsp matcha powder
- 60 grams sugar
- 120 ml milk
- 50 ml vegetable oil

Instructions:
1. In a bowl, mix flour, matcha powder, sugar, baking powder, and salt.
2. In another bowl, whisk milk, egg, and vegetable oil.
3. Combine the wet and dry Ingredients. Fold in white chocolate chips.
4. Preheat the Ninja Air Fryer to 180°C.
5. Pour the mixture into muffin moulds, filling them ¾ of the way.
6. Place the moulds in the air fryer and cook for 15 minutes or until a toothpick comes out clean.

Air Fried Peri-Peri Chicken Breakfast Wraps (African-inspired)

Prep time: 20 minutes   Cooking Time: 15 minutes   Servings: 4

Ingredients:
- 4 small tortilla wraps
- 2 tbsp peri-peri sauce (adjust to taste)
- 1 small red onion, thinly sliced
- Fresh coriander, chopped
- 200 grams chicken breast, thinly sliced
- 1 bell pepper, thinly sliced
- 50 grams feta cheese, crumbled
- 30 ml olive oil

Instructions:
1. In a bowl, marinate chicken slices with peri-peri sauce for at least 10 minutes.
2. Preheat the Ninja Air Fryer to 180°C.
3. Place the marinated chicken slices in the air fryer and cook for 12 minutes or until fully cooked.
4. Lay out tortilla wraps, place cooked chicken, bell pepper slices, red onion, crumbled feta, and fresh coriander in the center.
5. Roll up the wraps tightly, brush the outside with olive oil.
6. Place the wraps back in the air fryer and cook for an additional 3 minutes until crispy.

Air Fried Apricot & Pistachio Granola Bars (Middle Eastern-inspired)

Prep time: 20 minutes Cooking Time: 15 minutes Servings: 4

Ingredients:
- 150 grams rolled oats
- 50 grams pistachios, chopped
- 2 tbsp coconut oil, melted
- A pinch of salt
- 100 grams dried apricots, chopped
- 3 tbsp honey
- 1 tsp rose water (optional)

Instructions:
1. In a bowl, combine rolled oats, chopped apricots, and pistachios.
2. Mix in honey, melted coconut oil, rose water, and salt until well combined.
3. Press the mixture into a rectangular shape on a parchment-lined tray.
4. Preheat the Ninja Air Fryer to 180°C.
5. Place the granola mixture in the air fryer and cook for 15 minutes or until golden and set.
6. Allow to cool and then slice into bars.

Air Fried Corn & Zucchini Fritters (Australian-inspired)

Prep time: 25 minutes Cooking Time: 15 minutes Servings: 4

Ingredients:
- 1 zucchini, grated
- 100 grams all-purpose flour
- 50 ml milk
- Fresh chives, chopped
- 30 ml olive oil
- 150 grams corn kernels
- 1 large egg
- 1 tsp baking powder
- Salt and pepper to taste

Instructions:
1. In a bowl, combine grated zucchini, corn kernels, and chopped chives.
2. In another bowl, whisk together flour, egg, milk, baking powder, salt, and pepper to form a batter.
3. Mix the vegetables into the batter until well combined.
4. Preheat the Ninja Air Fryer to 180°C.
5. Drop spoonfuls of the batter into the air fryer, flattening them slightly.
6. Cook for 15 minutes or until golden and crispy, flipping halfway through.

Air Fried Potato & Sauerkraut Pierogi (Eastern European-inspired)

Prep time: 40 minutes Cooking Time: 15 minutes Servings: 4

Ingredients:
- 200 grams pierogi dough (or ready-made wrappers)
- 150 grams potatoes, boiled and mashed
- 1 small onion, finely chopped
- Salt and pepper to taste
- 50 grams sauerkraut, drained
- 30 ml olive oil
- Sour cream for serving

Instructions:
1. In a pan, sauté onions in a tablespoon of olive oil until translucent.
2. Combine mashed potatoes, sauerkraut, onions, salt, and pepper in a bowl.
3. Roll out the pierogi dough and cut into circles. Fill each circle with the potato mixture and seal the edges.
4. Brush each pierogi with olive oil.
5. Preheat the Ninja Air Fryer to 180°C.
6. Place the pierogi in the air fryer and cook for 15 minutes or until golden brown, turning halfway.

Air Fried Banana & Nutella Spring Rolls
(Southeast Asian-inspired with a twist)

Prep time: 20 minutesCooking Time: 10 minutesServings: 4

Ingredients:
- 8 spring roll wrappers
- Icing sugar for dusting
- 2 ripe bananas, sliced
- 30 ml vegetable oil
- 100 grams Nutella spread

Instructions:
1. Lay out the spring roll wrappers. Place banana slices on each wrapper and top with a dollop of Nutella.
2. Roll the wrappers tightly, sealing the edges.
3. Brush each spring roll with vegetable oil.
4. Preheat the Ninja Air Fryer to 180°C.
5. Place the spring rolls in the air fryer and cook for 10 minutes or until crispy and golden.
6. Dust with icing sugar before serving.

Air Fried Stuffed Tomato & Tuna Peppers
(Mediterranean-inspired)

Prep time: 20 minutesCooking Time: 12 minutesServings: 4

Ingredients:
- 4 large bell peppers, tops removed and deseeded
- 2 large tomatoes, diced
- 2 tbsp capers
- 30 ml olive oil
- 200 grams canned tuna, drained
- 50 grams olives, chopped
- 2 tbsp fresh parsley, chopped
- Salt and pepper to taste

Instructions:
1. In a bowl, mix together tuna, tomatoes, olives, capers, parsley, salt, and pepper.
2. Stuff each bell pepper with the tuna mixture.
3. Brush the outside of the peppers with olive oil.
4. Preheat the Ninja Air Fryer to 180°C.
5. Place the stuffed peppers in the air fryer and cook for 12 minutes or until the peppers are tender.
6. Drizzle with extra olive oil and sprinkle with fresh parsley before serving.

Air Fried Chorizo & Egg Breakfast Pockets (Mexican-inspired)

Prep time: 20 minutes Cooking Time: 15 minutes Servings: 4

Ingredients:
- 4 pocket pitas
- 4 large eggs, scrambled
- 1 small red onion, finely chopped
- 30 ml olive oil
- 200 grams chorizo, crumbled
- 50 grams cheddar cheese, grated
- Fresh cilantro, chopped
- Salsa for serving

Instructions:
1. In a pan, cook the crumbled chorizo until browned. Add onions and cook until translucent.
2. Mix in the scrambled eggs and cook until just set.
3. Stuff each pita pocket with the chorizo and egg mixture, and sprinkle with cheddar cheese and cilantro.
4. Brush the outside of the pita pockets with olive oil.
5. Preheat the Ninja Air Fryer to 180°C.
6. Place the stuffed pitas in the air fryer and cook for 15 minutes or until crispy and golden.
7. Serve with salsa on the side.

Air Fried Lamb & Mint Breakfast Sausages (British-inspired)

Prep time: 30 minutes (excluding resting time) Cooking Time: 12 minutes Servings: 4

Ingredients:
- 300 grams ground lamb
- 1 small onion, finely grated
- 1 tsp ground coriander
- Sausage casings
- 2 tbsp fresh mint, finely chopped
- 1 garlic clove, minced
- Salt and pepper to taste

Instructions:
1. In a bowl, mix together ground lamb, mint, onion, garlic, coriander, salt, and pepper.
2. Stuff the lamb mixture into sausage casings, forming individual sausages.
3. Allow sausages to rest in the refrigerator for an hour.
4. Preheat the Ninja Air Fryer to 180°C.
5. Place the lamb sausages in the air fryer and cook for 12 minutes or until browned and fully cooked, turning halfway.

Pancakes

Serves: 5 pancakes Prep time: 5 mins Cook time: 6 - 8 mins

Ingredients:
- 200 g plain flour
- 360 ml buttermilk
- 1 tsp baking powder
- ½ tsp salt
- 1 egg
- 1 tbsp sugar

Preparation Procedures:
1. Mix flour, baking powder, sugar and salt in a mixing bowl.
2. Melt the butter over a medium / low heat.

3. Beat the egg in a small bowl, pour in milk and melted butter and mix well.
4. Preheat your airfryer to 180°C.
5. Grease a small cake tin (choose a size that will fit in your airfryer basket)
6. Pour enough batter for one pancake into the tin.
7. Put tin in oven and cook in air fryer for 6 - 8 minutes ~ (until golden brown colour)
8. Serve with a choice of topping.

Air Fryer Banana Pancakes

Servings: 2   Prep time: 18 mins   Cook Time: 8 mins

Ingredients
- 1 large ripe banana
- ½ tablespoon of cooking oil (vegetable, avocado or coconut oil)
- 200g Flour
- 1 tsp Baking powder
- A pinch of salt
- 1 large egg
- 120g Sugar
- Milk
- Lemon juice / Buttermilk (optional)

Preparation Procedure
1. In a bowl, mash ripe banana until smooth. Ensure the banana is super ripe to add sweetness and depth to the pancake. Press into the banana using a fork and mash thoroughly.
2. Add egg and combine thoroughly with the mashed bananas. Do this until you have a smooth mixture.
3. Add the flour, baking powder, milk, and a pinch of salt to the bowl and mix until well combined.
4. To get your pancakes fluffy, increase the acidity of the pancake mix. You can get this with the addition of lemon juice or using buttermilk as it is also acidic
5. Turn on your Ninja Dual Zone Air Fryer and select the "AIR FRY" option.
6. Preheat the Ninja Dual Zone Air Fryer to 175°C.
7. Lightly grease the air fryer basket or use parchment paper.
8. Spoon small portions of the pancake batter onto the prepared basket.
9. Cook for 4-5 minutes, flip the pancakes, and cook for 2-3 minutes.
10. Serve the pancakes warm with your favorite toppings.

Chapter 2 Lunch

Air Fryer Italian Margherita Flatbread

Prep time: 10 minutes   Cooking Time: 8 minutes   Servings: 2

Ingredients:
- 150g pizza dough
- 2 tomatoes, sliced
- 1 tbsp olive oil
- 100g mozzarella cheese, sliced
- Fresh basil leaves
- Salt to taste

Instructions:
1. Roll out the pizza dough into a thin rectangle.
2. Top with mozzarella slices, tomato slices, and fresh basil.
3. Drizzle with olive oil and sprinkle with salt.
4. Air fry at 200°C for 8 minutes or until crispy.

Air Fryer French Croque Monsieur

Prep time: 15 minutes   Cooking Time: 7 minutes   Servings: 2

Ingredients:
- 4 slices of bread
- 100g Gruyère cheese, grated
- 1 tsp mustard
- 100g ham slices
- 150ml béchamel sauce
- Salt and pepper to taste

Instructions:
1. Spread mustard on two slices of bread. Top with ham and half of the cheese.
2. Close sandwiches with the remaining bread slices.
3. Spread béchamel sauce on top and sprinkle with the remaining cheese.
4. Air fry at 190°C for 7 minutes or until golden brown.

Air Fryer Chinese Vegetable Spring Rolls

Prep time: 20 minutes   Cooking Time: 10 minutes   Servings: 4

Ingredients:
- 8 spring roll wrappers
- 50g carrots, julienned
- 2 green onions, chopped
- 1 tsp ginger, minced
- 100g cabbage, finely shredded
- 50g bell peppers, julienned
- 2 tbsp soy sauce

Instructions:
1. Sauté vegetables with ginger until tender. Add soy sauce and cool.
2. Place the mixture on each wrapper and roll tightly, sealing edges with water.
3. Air fry at 190°C for 10 minutes or until golden brown.

Air Fryer Greek Spanakorizo (Spinach Rice)

Prep time: 10 minutes Cooking Time: 20 minutes Servings: 3

Ingredients:
- 150g rice
- 1 onion, finely chopped
- 500ml vegetable broth
- 1 lemon, zested and juiced
- 200g fresh spinach, chopped
- 2 cloves garlic, minced
- 2 tbsp olive oil
- Salt and pepper to taste

Instructions:
1. Sauté onions and garlic in olive oil. Add rice and stir.
2. Add vegetable broth, spinach, lemon zest, and juice.
3. Transfer to an air fryer-safe dish and air fry at 160°C for 20 minutes or until rice is cooked.

Air Fryer Indian Aloo Tikki (Potato Patties)

Prep time: 20 minutes Cooking Time: 15 minutes Servings: 4

Ingredients:
- 300g potatoes, boiled and mashed
- 1 green chilli, finely chopped
- 1 tsp cumin powder
- Fresh coriander, chopped
- 50g peas, boiled
- 2 tsp coriander powder
- Salt to taste

Instructions:
1. Mix all Ingredients together and shape into patties.
2. Air fry at 190°C for 15 minutes or until golden brown.

Air Fryer American BBQ Chicken Sliders

Prep time: 10 minutes Cooking Time: 15 minutes Servings: 4

Ingredients:
- 300g chicken breast, cooked and shredded
- 8 mini slider buns
- 150ml BBQ sauce
- 50g coleslaw

Instructions:
1. Mix shredded chicken with BBQ sauce.
2. Air fry at 160°C for 7 minutes to heat.
3. Assemble sliders with chicken mixture and top with coleslaw.

Air Fryer Moroccan Vegetable Tagine

Prep time: 15 minutes Cooking Time: 25 minutes Servings: 4

Ingredients:
- 200g carrots, chopped
- 100g dried apricots, chopped
- 1 tsp cumin powder
- 200g zucchini, chopped
- 2 tbsp olive oil
- 1 tsp paprika

- 500ml vegetable broth
- Fresh coriander, chopped
- Salt to taste

Instructions:
1. Sauté vegetables and apricots with spices in olive oil.
2. Add vegetable broth and transfer to an air fryer-safe dish.
3. Air fry at 160°C for 25 minutes or until vegetables are tender.

Air Fryer Turkish Gözleme (Stuffed Flatbread)

Prep time: 20 minutes Cooking Time: 10 minutes Servings: 4

Ingredients:
- 300g flour
- 200g spinach, chopped
- 1 onion, finely chopped
- Olive oil for brushing
- 150ml water
- 100g feta cheese, crumbled
- 1 tsp paprika
- Salt to taste

Instructions:
1. Mix flour and water to form a dough. Divide into balls.
2. Sauté onions, spinach, and paprika. Mix with feta cheese.
3. Roll each dough ball into a thin circle, place the filling, and fold.
4. Brush with olive oil and air fry at 190°C for 10 minutes or until golden.

Air Fryer Japanese Teriyaki Salmon Bowl

Prep time: 15 minutes Cooking Time: 12 minutes Servings: 2

Ingredients:
- 2 salmon fillets
- 200g cooked jasmine rice
- 1 tbsp sesame seeds
- 100ml teriyaki sauce
- 2 green onions, chopped
- Fresh coriander for garnish

Instructions:
1. Marinate salmon fillets in teriyaki sauce for 10 minutes.
2. Air fry at 180°C for 12 minutes or until salmon is cooked through.
3. Serve over jasmine rice, garnish with green onions, sesame seeds, and fresh coriander.

Air Fryer Brazilian Pão de Queijo (Cheese Bread)

Prep time: 20 minutes Cooking Time: 10 minutes Servings: 6

Ingredients:
- 250g tapioca flour
- 50g butter
- 150g Parmesan cheese, grated
- 150ml milk
- 1 tsp salt
- 2 beaten eggs

Instructions:
1. Heat milk, butter, and salt until milk is hot and butter is melted. Stir in tapioca flour until thoroughly combined.

2. Let the mixture rest for 15 minutes.
3. Add cheese and beaten eggs. Mix until smooth.
4. Shape into small balls and air fry at 190°C for 10 minutes or until lightly golden.

Air Fryer Kenyan Samosas

Prep time: 30 minutes   Cooking Time: 15 minutes   Servings: 4

Ingredients:
- 200g minced beef or chicken
- 2 cloves garlic, minced
- 1 tsp cumin powder
- 50g carrots, finely diced
- Salt to taste
- 1 onion, finely chopped
- 1 tsp curry powder
- 50g peas
- 8 samosa wrappers

Instructions:
1. Sauté onions, garlic, and meat until browned. Add spices, peas, and carrots. Cook until vegetables are tender.
2. Place a spoonful of the mixture on each wrapper, fold into triangles, and seal edges with water.
3. Air fry at 190°C for 15 minutes or until golden brown.

Air Fryer Spanish Tortilla (Potato Omelette)

Prep time: 20 minutes   Cooking Time: 15 minutes   Servings: 4

Ingredients:
- 300g potatoes, thinly sliced
- 6 eggs, beaten
- Salt and pepper to taste
- 1 onion, thinly sliced
- 50ml olive oil

Instructions:
1. Sauté potatoes and onion in olive oil until tender. Season with salt and pepper.
2. Add beaten eggs and mix.
3. Transfer to an air fryer-safe dish and air fry at 180°C for 15 minutes or until set.

Air Fryer Vietnamese Bánh Mì Sandwich

Prep time: 20 minutes   Cooking Time: 10 minutes   Servings: 2

Ingredients:
- 2 baguette rolls
- 50g carrots, julienned
- 2 tbsp rice vinegar
- Fresh coriander, mint, and jalapeño slices
- 2 tbsp mayonnaise
- 100g cooked pork or chicken, thinly sliced
- 50g radishes, julienned
- 1 tbsp sugar
- 1 tsp soy sauce

Instructions:
1. Mix carrots, radishes, rice vinegar, and sugar. Let sit for 10 minutes to pickle.
2. Mix mayonnaise and soy sauce.
3. Assemble sandwiches with meat, pickled vegetables, herbs, jalapeños, and mayo mixture.

Air Fryer Lebanese Falafel Wrap

Prep time: 30 minutes   Cooking Time: 15 minutes   Servings: 4

Ingredients:
- 200g chickpeas, soaked overnight and drained
- 2 cloves garlic, minced
- 1 tsp coriander powder
- 4 tortilla wraps
- 50ml tahini sauce
- 1 onion, chopped
- 2 tsp cumin powder
- Fresh coriander and parsley, chopped
- Fresh lettuce, tomatoes, and cucumbers

Instructions:
1. Blend chickpeas, onion, garlic, spices, and herbs until a coarse mixture forms. Shape into balls.
2. Air fry at 190°C for 15 minutes or until golden brown.
3. Assemble wraps with falafels, vegetables, and tahini sauce.

Air Fryer Thai Basil Chicken

Prep time: 15 minutes   Cooking Time: 10 minutes   Servings: 2

Ingredients:
- 200g chicken breast, thinly sliced
- 2 cloves garlic, minced
- 2 tbsp soy sauce
- 2 tbsp vegetable oil
- 50g fresh basil leaves
- 2 red chillies, sliced
- 1 tbsp oyster sauce

Instructions:
1. Sauté garlic and chillies in vegetable oil until aromatic.
2. Add chicken slices and cook until browned.
3. Mix in soy sauce and oyster sauce, cooking until chicken is glazed.
4. Stir in basil leaves until wilted.
5. Transfer to an air fryer-safe dish and air fry at 180°C for 10 minutes.

Grilled Chicken Fajitas

Prep time: 10 minutes   Cook time: 20 minutes   Serves: 4

Ingredients:
- 500 g of boneless, skinless chicken breasts, sliced into thin strips
- 2 bell peppers, sliced into thin strips
- 2 tbsp olive oil
- Salt and pepper, to taste
- Optional toppings: shredded cheese, sour cream, guacamole, salsa
- 1 onion, sliced into thin strips
- 2 tbsp taco seasoning
- Flour or corn tortillas

Instructions:
1. Preheat the Ninja Dual Zone to Air Fry mode at 190°C for 5 minutes.
2. In a large bowl, toss the chicken strips with 1 tbsp of olive oil and taco seasoning until evenly coated.
3. Place the chicken strips in the basket of the Ninja Dual Zone and cook for 8-10 minutes, or

until cooked through, flipping halfway through.
4. Remove the chicken from the basket and set aside.
5. In the same bowl, toss the sliced peppers and onions with the remaining 1 tbsp of olive oil, salt, and pepper.
6. Place the pepper and onion mixture in the basket of the Ninja Dual Zone and cook for 6-8 minutes, or until they are tender and slightly charred, stirring halfway through.
7. Add the cooked chicken back to the basket and toss everything together to combine.
8. Serve the fajita mixture with warm tortillas and any desired toppings.

Spinach and Feta Stuffed Chicken

Serves: 4 Prep time: 15 minutes Cook time: 18-20 minutes

Ingredients:
- 4 boneless, skinless chicken breasts
- 125 ml of crumbled feta cheese
- 1 teaspoon garlic powder
- 1/2 teaspoon dried basil
- 250 ml of fresh spinach leaves, chopped
- 2 tablespoons olive oil
- 1/2 teaspoon onion powder
- Salt and pepper, to taste

Instructions:
1. Preheat your Ninja Dual Zone to Air Fry mode at 190°C.
2. In a bowl, mix the chopped spinach, crumbled feta cheese, olive oil, garlic powder, onion powder, dried basil, salt, and pepper.
3. Cut a pocket into each chicken breast by slicing horizontally through the thickest part, but not all the way through.
4. Stuff each chicken breast with the spinach and feta mixture, then use toothpicks to secure the opening.
5. Place the stuffed chicken breasts in the Vortex Plus Ninja Dual basket and air fry for 18-20 minutes, flipping halfway through, until the chicken is cooked through and golden brown.
6. Remove the toothpicks from the chicken and serve hot.

Chapter 3 Diner

Air Fryer French Coq au Vin

Prep time: 20 minutes   Cooking Time: 25 minutes   Servings: 4

Ingredients:
- 4 chicken thighs
- 1 onion, chopped
- 2 tbsp olive oil
- 200ml red wine
- 150g button mushrooms, sliced
- Salt and pepper to taste
- 2 cloves garlic, minced
- 2 carrots, sliced

Instructions:
1. Sauté onion and garlic in olive oil until translucent. Add chicken thighs and brown on all sides.
2. Add red wine, mushrooms, and carrots. Allow the mixture to simmer until the wine reduces by half.
3. Transfer to an air fryer-safe dish and air fry at 180°C for 25 minutes or until the chicken is cooked through.

Air Fryer Indian Butter Chicken

Prep time: 20 minutes   Cooking Time: 20 minutes   Servings: 4

Ingredients:
- 400g chicken breast, diced
- 2 tbsp butter
- 1 tsp chili powder
- 150ml tomato puree
- 2 tsp garam masala
- Salt to taste
- 100ml heavy cream
- 1 tsp turmeric
- Fresh coriander for garnish

Instructions:
1. Melt butter in a pan, add garam masala, turmeric, and chili powder. Stir until aromatic.
2. Add chicken pieces and brown on all sides.
3. Mix in tomato puree and simmer for 10 minutes.
4. Stir in heavy cream and cook until heated through.
5. Transfer to an air fryer-safe dish and air fry at 180°C for 20 minutes.
6. Garnish with fresh coriander before serving.

Air Fryer Moroccan Lamb Tagine

Prep time: 30 minutes   Cooking Time: 35 minutes   Servings: 4

Ingredients:
- 400g lamb, diced
- 100g dried apricots, chopped
- 2 tsp coriander
- Salt to taste
- 1 onion, chopped
- 50g almonds, toasted
- 250ml beef or lamb broth
- 2 cloves garlic, minced
- 2 tsp cumin
- Olive oil for frying

Instructions:
1. Sauté onion and garlic in olive oil. Add lamb pieces and brown.
2. Stir in cumin, coriander, apricots, almonds, and broth.

3. Transfer to an air fryer-safe dish and air fry at 180°C for 35 minutes or until lamb is tender.

Air Fryer Chinese Kung Pao Chicken

Prep time: 20 minutes Cooking Time: 20 minutes Servings: 4

Ingredients:
- 400g chicken breast, diced
- 4 dried red chilies
- 1 tsp sesame oil
- 50g roasted peanuts
- 2 tbsp soy sauce
- 1 tbsp sugar
- 2 bell peppers, diced
- 1 tbsp rice vinegar
- Olive oil for frying

Instructions:
1. In a pan, sauté chicken pieces in olive oil until browned. Remove and set aside.
2. In the same pan, fry dried red chilies and bell peppers.
3. Add back the chicken, then stir in soy sauce, rice vinegar, sesame oil, and sugar.
4. Toss in roasted peanuts and stir well.
5. Transfer to an air fryer-safe dish and air fry at 190°C for 20 minutes.

Air Fryer Mexican Chili Con Carne

Prep time: 20 minutes Cooking Time: 30 minutes Servings: 4

Ingredients:
- 400g minced beef
- 400g canned red kidney beans, drained
- 2 tsp chili powder
- Fresh cilantro for garnish
- 1 onion, chopped
- 1 tsp cumin
- 2 cloves garlic, minced
- 400g canned diced tomatoes
- Salt to taste

Instructions:
1. Sauté onion and garlic until translucent. Add minced beef and brown.
2. Stir in chili powder, cumin, beans, and diced tomatoes. Simmer for 10 minutes.
3. Transfer to an air fryer-safe dish and air fry at 180°C for 30 minutes.
4. Garnish with fresh cilantro before serving.

Air Fryer Japanese Teriyaki Salmon

Prep time: 15 minutes Cooking Time: 20 minutes Servings: 4

Ingredients:
- 4 salmon fillets
- 50ml sake
- Sliced green onions for garnish
- 100ml soy sauce
- 4 tbsp sugar
- 50ml mirin
- 1 tbsp sesame seeds

Instructions:
1. In a pan, combine soy sauce, mirin, sake, and sugar. Simmer until reduced to a thick glaze.
2. Brush salmon fillets with the teriyaki glaze.
3. Air fry at 180°C for 20 minutes or until salmon is cooked to your liking.
4. Garnish with sesame seeds and green onions.

Air Fryer Brazilian Picanha Steak

Prep time: 10 minutes Cooking Time: 15 minutes Servings: 4

Ingredients:
- 800g picanha steak (rump cap)
- Coarse salt to taste
- Lime wedges for serving

Instructions:
1. Generously season the picanha steak with coarse salt.
2. Air fry at 190°C for 15 minutes or until the steak reaches your desired doneness.
3. Rest for a few minutes, then slice against the grain.
4. Serve with lime wedges.

Air Fryer Greek Moussaka

Prep time: 30 minutes Cooking Time: 40 minutes Servings: 4

Ingredients:
- 2 large eggplants, sliced
- 2 cloves garlic, minced
- 50g butter
- 100g grated Parmesan cheese
- 400g minced lamb or beef
- 400g canned tomatoes
- 50g flour
- Olive oil for frying
- 1 onion, chopped
- 2 tsp oregano
- 500ml milk
- Salt and pepper to taste

Instructions:
1. Fry eggplant slices in olive oil until golden. Set aside.
2. In the same pan, sauté onion and garlic. Add minced meat and brown. Stir in tomatoes and oregano. Simmer for 10 minutes.
3. In another pan, melt butter and stir in flour. Gradually add milk, stirring continuously until a thick sauce forms. Season with salt, pepper, and half of the Parmesan.
4. In an air fryer-safe dish, layer eggplant slices, meat mixture, and béchamel sauce. Repeat layers and top with remaining Parmesan.
5. Air fry at 180°C for 40 minutes or until golden and bubbly.

Air Fryer Kenyan Sukuma Wiki

Prep time: 10 minutes Cooking Time: 20 minutes Servings: 4

Ingredients:
- 400g collard greens, chopped
- 2 cloves garlic, minced
- Olive oil for frying
- 2 tomatoes, diced
- 1 tsp cumin
- Salt to taste
- 1 onion, chopped
- 1 tsp coriander

Instructions:
1. Sauté onions and garlic in olive oil until translucent. Add tomatoes and cook until soft.
2. Stir in collard greens, cumin, and coriander. Cook until greens are tender.
3. Transfer to an air fryer-safe dish and air fry at 180°C for 20 minutes.

Air Fryer Turkish Kofta Kebabs

Prep time: 20 minutes Cooking Time: 15 minutes Servings: 4

Ingredients:
- 400g minced beef or lamb
- 2 tsp paprika
- Salt and pepper to taste
- 1 onion, grated
- 1 tsp cumin
- 2 cloves garlic, minced
- Fresh parsley, chopped

Instructions:
1. Mix minced meat, onion, garlic, spices, and parsley. Shape into long kebabs around skewers.
2. Air fry at 190°C for 15 minutes or until kebabs are browned and cooked through.

Air Fryer Peruvian Lomo Saltado

Prep time: 25 minutes   Cooking Time: 20 minutes   Servings: 4

Ingredients:
- 400g beef strips
- 2 tomatoes, wedges
- 50ml soy sauce
- Olive oil for frying
- 300g potatoes, cut into fries
- 2 chili peppers, sliced
- 2 tbsp red wine vinegar
- Salt and pepper to taste
- 1 red onion, sliced
- 3 cloves garlic, minced
- Fresh cilantro, chopped

Instructions:
1. Air fry the potato fries at 190°C for 15 minutes or until crispy.
2. In a pan, sauté beef strips in olive oil until browned. Remove and set aside.
3. In the same pan, fry onions, tomatoes, chili peppers, and garlic.
4. Return the beef to the pan. Pour in soy sauce and vinegar, stirring well.
5. Mix in the air-fried potatoes and garnish with cilantro.

Air Fryer German Bratwurst with Sauerkraut

Prep time: 10 minutes   Cooking Time: 20 minutes   Servings: 4

Ingredients:
- 4 bratwurst sausages
- 1 onion, sliced
- Olive oil for frying
- 400g sauerkraut
- 2 tbsp mustard
- Salt and pepper to taste
- 1 apple, sliced
- 100ml beer (optional)

Instructions:
1. Air fry the bratwurst sausages at 180°C for 15 minutes or until browned and cooked through.
2. In a pan, sauté onions and apple slices in olive oil until soft. Add sauerkraut, mustard, and beer. Simmer for 10 minutes.
3. Serve the bratwurst with the sauerkraut mixture.

Air Fryer Ghanaian Kelewele (Spicy Fried Plantains)

Prep time: 15 minutes   Cooking Time: 20 minutes   Servings: 4

Ingredients:
- 4 ripe plantains, diced
- 1 tsp ground ginger
- 2 tsp ground cayenne pepper
- Salt to taste

Instructions:
1. Toss plantain pieces with cayenne, ginger, and salt.

2. Air fry at 190°C for 20 minutes or until the plantains are golden and crispy.

Air Fryer Italian Eggplant Parmesan

Prep time: 20 minutes Cooking Time: 30 minutes Servings: 4

Ingredients:
- 2 large eggplants, sliced
- 100g Parmesan cheese, grated
- 2 eggs, beaten
- Fresh basil leaves
- Salt and pepper to taste
- 200g mozzarella cheese, sliced
- 400g tomato sauce
- 200g breadcrumbs
- Olive oil for brushing

Instructions:
1. Dip eggplant slices in beaten eggs, then coat with breadcrumbs.
2. Air fry the breaded eggplant slices at 190°C for 10 minutes or until crispy.
3. In an air fryer-safe dish, layer eggplant, tomato sauce, mozzarella, and Parmesan. Repeat layers until all Ingredients are used.
4. Air fry at 180°C for 20 minutes or until bubbly and golden.
5. Garnish with fresh basil leaves.

Air Fryer Thai Basil Chicken

Prep time: 15 minutes Cooking Time: 20 minutes Servings: 4

Ingredients:
- 400g chicken breast, minced
- 50g fresh Thai basil leaves
- 1 tsp sugar
- 2 cloves garlic, minced
- 2 tbsp soy sauce
- Olive oil for frying
- 2 chili peppers, sliced
- 1 tbsp oyster sauce

Instructions:
1. Sauté garlic and chili peppers in olive oil until aromatic. Add minced chicken and brown.
2. Stir in soy sauce, oyster sauce, and sugar.
3. Just before removing from heat, mix in fresh basil leaves until wilted.
4. Transfer to an air fryer-safe dish and air fry at 180°C for 20 minutes.

Air Fryer Russian Beef Stroganoff

Prep time: 20 minutes Cooking Time: 25 minutes Servings: 4

Ingredients:
- 400g beef strips
- 2 cloves garlic, minced
- 2 tbsp olive oil
- 200g mushrooms, sliced
- 250ml sour cream
- Salt and pepper to taste
- 1 onion, finely chopped
- 50ml beef broth
- Fresh dill for garnish

Instructions:
1. Sauté onions and garlic in olive oil until translucent. Add beef strips and brown on all sides.
2. Add mushrooms and continue cooking until softened.
3. Pour in beef broth and simmer for 10 minutes.
4. Stir in sour cream, ensuring it doesn't boil. Season with salt and pepper.

5. Transfer to an air fryer-safe dish and air fry at 180°C for 25 minutes.
6. Garnish with fresh dill before serving.

Air Fryer Filipino Chicken Adobo

Prep time: 15 minutes (plus marinating time) Cooking Time: 30 minutes Servings: 4

Ingredients:
- 4 chicken thighs
- 3 cloves garlic, smashed
- 1 tbsp sugar
- 100ml soy sauce
- 2 bay leaves
- 2 tbsp olive oil
- 75ml white vinegar
- 1 tsp black peppercorns

Instructions:
1. In a bowl, combine soy sauce, vinegar, garlic, bay leaves, peppercorns, and sugar. Marinate chicken thighs for at least 2 hours.
2. Heat olive oil in a pan and brown the chicken on all sides.
3. Add the marinade and simmer until reduced by half.
4. Transfer chicken and sauce to an air fryer-safe dish and air fry at 190°C for 30 minutes or until chicken is cooked through.

Air Fryer Spanish Patatas Bravas

Prep time: 15 minutes Cooking Time: 25 minutes Servings: 4

Ingredients:
- 400g potatoes, diced
- 1 tsp smoked paprika
- Salt to taste
- 200g canned tomatoes
- 1 tsp chili powder
- 2 cloves garlic, minced
- 2 tbsp olive oil

Instructions:
1. Air fry potatoes at 190°C for 20 minutes or until golden and crispy.
2. In a pan, heat olive oil and sauté garlic. Add tomatoes, smoked paprika, chili powder, and salt. Simmer until thickened.
3. Pour the sauce over the crispy potatoes.

Air Fryer Korean Bulgogi

Prep time: 15 minutes (plus marinating time) Cooking Time: 20 minutes Servings: 4

Ingredients:
- 400g beef slices
- 1 tbsp mirin
- 1 onion, sliced
- Toasted sesame seeds for garnish
- 50ml soy sauce
- 2 cloves garlic, minced
- 2 green onions, chopped
- 2 tbsp sugar
- 1 small pear, grated
- 1 tbsp toasted sesame oil

Instructions:
1. Combine soy sauce, sugar, mirin, garlic, and grated pear in a bowl. Marinate beef slices for at least 1 hour.
2. In a pan, heat sesame oil and sauté onions until translucent. Add marinated beef and cook until browned.
3. Transfer to an air fryer-safe dish and air fry at 190°C for 20 minutes.
4. Garnish with chopped green onions and toasted sesame seeds.

Air Fryer Hungarian Goulash

Prep time: 20 minutes   Cooking Time: 40 minutes   Servings: 4

Ingredients:
- 400g beef cubes
- 3 cloves garlic, minced
- 400g canned tomatoes
- Salt and pepper to taste
- 2 onions, chopped
- 3 tbsp paprika
- 250ml beef broth
- 2 bell peppers, diced
- 1 tsp caraway seeds
- 2 tbsp olive oil

Instructions:
1. Sauté onions and garlic in olive oil until translucent. Add beef cubes and brown on all sides.
2. Stir in paprika, caraway seeds, bell peppers, tomatoes, and beef broth. Simmer until beef is tender.
3. Transfer to an air fryer-safe dish and air fry at 180°C for 40 minutes.

Air Fryer Moroccan Lamb Tagine

Prep time: 30 minutes   Cooking Time: 40 minutes   Servings: 4

Ingredients:
- 400g lamb cubes
- 100g dried apricots, halved
- 2 tsp ground coriander
- 2 tbsp olive oil
- 2 onions, finely chopped
- 50g slivered almonds
- 1 tsp ground cinnamon
- Fresh coriander for garnish
- 2 cloves garlic, minced
- 2 tsp ground cumin
- 400ml chicken broth
- Salt and pepper to taste

Instructions:
1. Sauté onions and garlic in olive oil until translucent. Add lamb cubes and brown on all sides.
2. Stir in cumin, coriander, and cinnamon. Add dried apricots, almonds, and chicken broth. Let it simmer until lamb is tender.
3. Transfer to an air fryer-safe dish and air fry at 180°C for 40 minutes.
4. Garnish with fresh coriander before serving.

Air Fryer Indian Butter Chicken

Prep time: 20 minutes   Cooking Time: 30 minutes   Servings: 4

Ingredients:
- 400g chicken breast, cubed
- 2 onions, finely chopped
- 1 tsp turmeric
- Fresh cilantro for garnish
- 200ml heavy cream
- 3 cloves garlic, minced
- 1 tsp chili powder
- Salt to taste
- 200g tomato puree
- 2 tsp garam masala
- 2 tbsp butter

Instructions:
1. Melt butter in a pan and sauté onions and garlic until translucent.
2. Add chicken cubes and brown on all sides.
3. Stir in garam masala, turmeric, and chili powder. Add tomato puree and let it simmer until chicken is cooked through.
4. Stir in heavy cream and simmer for another 5 minutes.
5. Transfer to an air fryer-safe dish and air fry at 180°C for 30 minutes.
6. Garnish with fresh cilantro before serving.

Air Fryer British Shepherd's Pie

Prep time: 30 minutes Cooking Time: 35 minutes Servings: 4

Ingredients:
- 400g minced lamb
- 1 onion, chopped
- 2 tbsp tomato paste
- Salt and pepper to taste
- 400g potatoes, boiled and mashed
- 2 cloves garlic, minced
- 2 tbsp butter
- 2 carrots, diced
- 200ml beef broth
- 50ml milk

Instructions:
1. Sauté onions, carrots, and garlic in butter until softened.
2. Add minced lamb and brown. Stir in tomato paste.
3. Pour in beef broth and let it simmer until thickened.
4. In a separate bowl, mix mashed potatoes with milk, salt, and pepper.
5. In an air fryer-safe dish, layer the meat mixture at the bottom and top with mashed potatoes.
6. Air fry at 190°C for 35 minutes or until the top is golden.

Air Fryer Vietnamese Lemongrass Chicken

Prep time: 20 minutes (plus marinating time) Cooking Time: 25 minutes Servings: 4

Ingredients:
- 4 chicken thighs
- 2 tbsp fish sauce
- Fresh chili slices and cilantro for garnish
- 2 stalks lemongrass, minced
- 1 tbsp sugar
- 4 cloves garlic, minced
- 2 tbsp olive oil

Instructions:
1. In a bowl, combine lemongrass, garlic, fish sauce, sugar, and olive oil. Marinate chicken thighs for at least 2 hours.
2. Air fry the marinated chicken thighs at 190°C for 25 minutes or until browned and cooked through.
3. Garnish with chili slices and cilantro.

Air Fryer Jamaican Jerk Chicken

Prep time: 20 minutes (plus marinating time) Cooking Time: 30 minutes Servings: 4

Ingredients:
- 4 chicken legs
- 2 Scotch bonnet peppers, deseeded
- 1 tsp ground nutmeg
- 2 tbsp brown sugar
- 3 scallions, chopped
- 1 tsp ground cinnamon
- 1 tbsp thyme leaves
- 3 cloves garlic, minced
- 1 tbsp ground allspice
- 60ml soy sauce
- Salt and pepper to taste

Instructions:
1. Blend scallions, garlic, Scotch bonnet peppers, allspice, nutmeg, cinnamon, soy sauce, brown sugar, thyme, salt, and pepper to form a paste.
2. Marinate chicken legs in the paste for at least 4 hours.
3. Air fry the marinated chicken legs at 190°C for 30 minutes or until browned and cooked through.

Steak Diane

Prep time: 10 minutes   Cook time: 10- 15 minutes   Serves: 2

Ingredients:

- 2 beef tenderloin steaks, about 8 oz each
- 2 tablespoons unsalted butter
- 32g beef stock
- 2 tablespoons Dijon mustard
- Salt and pepper, to taste
- 1 tablespoon olive oil
- 32g finely chopped shallots
- 2 tablespoons Worcestershire sauce
- 32g heavy cream
- Chopped parsley, for garnish

Instructions:

1. Preheat the Ninja Dual Zone to Sear at 200°C (200°C).
2. Season the beef tenderloin steaks with salt and pepper on both sides.
3. Add the olive oil to the Ninja Dual and sear the steaks for 2-3 minutes on each side, or until well browned and cooked to your desired level of doneness.
4. Remove the steaks from the Ninja Dual and set them aside on a plate.
5. In the same pan, add the butter and shallots and cook for 1-2 minutes, or until softened.
6. Add the beef stock, Worcestershire sauce, and Dijon mustard to the pan and stir to combine.
7. Cook the sauce for 1-2 minutes, or until slightly reduced.
8. Add the heavy cream to the pan and cook for another minute, stirring constantly.
9. Season the sauce with salt and pepper to taste.
10. Return the cooked steaks to the pan and spoon the sauce over them.
11. Garnish the Steak Diane with chopped parsley and serve immediately.

Fish and Chips

Prep time: 20 minutes   Cook time: 12-15 minutes   Serves: 4-6

Ingredients:

- 4-6 white fish fillets (such as cod or haddock)
- 1 tsp salt
- 1/2 tsp paprika
- 1 large egg
- 2 tbsp olive oil
- 1/2 tsp black pepper
- 1/4 tsp cayenne pepper
- 4-6 large potatoes, cut into thick chips
- Salt and pepper, to taste
- 128g all-purpose flour
- 1/2 tsp garlic powder
- 250 ml of beer

Instructions:

1. Preheat your Ninja Dual Zone to Air Fry mode at 190°C (190°C).
2. In a large bowl, whisk together the flour, salt, black pepper, garlic powder, paprika, and cayenne pepper.
3. In a separate bowl, whisk together the beer and egg.
4. Dip each fish fillet into the beer mixture, then into the flour mixture, making sure to coat evenly.
5. Place the coated fish fillets onto the Air Fryer basket, making sure to leave some space in between.
6. In another bowl, toss the potato chips with the olive oil and salt and pepper to taste.
7. Place the potato chips in the Air Fryer basket next to the fish fillets.
8. Cook for 12-15 minutes, flipping the fish fillets and potato chips halfway through, until the fish is golden brown and cooked through, and the potato chips are crispy.
9. Serve hot with tartar sauce, lemon wedges, and your favourite sides.

Chapter 4 Beef, Pork and lamb

Air Fryer Argentinian Beef Empanadas

Prep time: 30 minutes Cooking Time: 15 minutes Servings: 4

Ingredients:
- 300g minced beef
- 3 tbsp green olives, sliced
- 1 tsp cumin
- Ready-made empanada dough
- 1 onion, finely chopped
- 2 tbsp chopped parsley
- 30g raisins
- 2 hard-boiled eggs, chopped
- 2 tsp paprika
- Salt and pepper to taste

Instructions:
1. Sauté onion until translucent, add minced beef and cook until browned. Mix in the seasonings, eggs, olives, and raisins.
2. Cut the dough into circles, fill with beef mixture, fold, and seal the edges.
3. Air fry at 190°C for 15 minutes, turning halfway.

Air Fryer Korean Pork Bulgogi

Prep time: 20 minutes (plus marinating time) Cooking Time: 12 minutes Servings: 4

Ingredients:
- 400g thinly sliced pork belly
- 1 tbsp gochujang (Korean chilli paste)
- 3 cloves garlic, minced
- 3 tbsp soy sauce
- 1 onion, sliced
- 2 tbsp brown sugar
- 1 tbsp sesame oil
- Green onions for garnish

Instructions:
1. Mix soy sauce, sugar, gochujang, sesame oil, and garlic. Marinate the pork in this mixture for at least 2 hours.
2. Place pork and onion slices in the air fryer.
3. Cook at 180°C for 12 minutes, flipping halfway.
4. Garnish with green onions.

Air Fryer Moroccan Lamb Tagine

Prep time: 25 minutes Cooking Time: 20 minutes Servings: 4

Ingredients:
- 400g lamb chunks
- 1 onion, chopped
- 2 tbsp almond slivers
- Fresh cilantro for garnish
- 2 tsp ras el hanout (Moroccan spice blend)
- 2 garlic cloves, minced
- 250ml lamb stock
- 150g dried apricots, halved
- Salt to taste

Instructions:
1. Season lamb with ras el hanout. In a pan, sauté onions and garlic until translucent, add lamb

and brown all sides.
2. Transfer lamb mixture to the air fryer, add apricots, almonds, and lamb stock.
3. Cook at 160°C for 20 minutes.
4. Garnish with fresh cilantro.

Air Fryer Texas BBQ Beef Ribs

Prep time: 15 minutes (plus marinating time) Cooking Time: 25 minutes Servings: 4

Ingredients:
- 4 beef ribs
- 4 tbsp BBQ sauce
- 1 tbsp smoked paprika
- 1 tsp cayenne pepper
- Salt and pepper to taste

Instructions:
1. Rub the ribs with smoked paprika, cayenne, salt, and pepper. Marinate for at least 3 hours.
2. Brush the ribs with BBQ sauce.
3. Air fry at 160°C for 25 minutes, brushing with more BBQ sauce halfway.

Air Fryer German Pork Schnitzel

Prep time: 20 minutes Cooking Time: 15 minutes Servings: 4

Ingredients:
- 4 pork cutlets
- 100g breadcrumbs
- 2 eggs, beaten
- 50g flour
- 1 tsp paprika
- Salt and pepper to taste
- Lemon wedges for serving

Instructions:
1. Season the cutlets with salt, pepper, and paprika. Dredge in flour, dip in beaten eggs, and coat with breadcrumbs.
2. Air fry at 190°C for 15 minutes, flipping halfway.
3. Serve with lemon wedges.

Air Fryer Filipino Beef Adobo

Prep time: 20 minutes (plus marinating time) Cooking Time: 20 minutes Servings: 4

Ingredients:
- 400g beef chunks
- 4 cloves garlic, minced
- 100ml soy sauce
- 50ml vinegar
- 1 bay leaf
- 1 tsp black peppercorns
- 250ml beef stock

Instructions:
1. Marinate beef in garlic, soy sauce, vinegar, bay leaf, and peppercorns for at least 2 hours.
2. Transfer beef and marinade to the air fryer, add beef stock.
3. Cook at 160°C for 20 minutes.

Air Fryer Italian Pork Saltimbocca

Prep time: 20 minutes Cooking Time: 12 minutes Servings: 4

Ingredients:
- 4 pork cutlets
- 50g flour
- 4 slices prosciutto
- Salt and pepper to taste
- 4 sage leaves
- Olive oil for drizzling

Instructions:
1. Season the pork cutlets with salt and pepper. Place a sage leaf on each cutlet and wrap with a slice of prosciutto.
2. Lightly dredge in flour.
3. Drizzle with olive oil and air fry at 180°C for 12 minutes.

Air Fryer Middle Eastern Lamb Kofta

Prep time: 25 minutes Cooking Time: 15 minutes Servings: 4

Ingredients:
- 400g minced lamb
- 2 tsp cumin
- Salt and pepper to taste
- 1 onion, finely chopped
- 2 tsp coriander
- Fresh cilantro for garnish
- 2 cloves garlic, minced
- 1 tsp paprika

Instructions:
1. Mix lamb, onion, garlic, spices, salt, and pepper.
2. Shape the mixture into elongated koftas around skewers.
3. Air fry at 180°C for 15 minutes, turning halfway.
4. Garnish with fresh cilantro.

Air Fryer Thai Beef Satay

Prep time: 25 minutes (plus marinating time) Cooking Time: 12 minutes Servings: 4

Ingredients:
- 400g beef sirloin, sliced into strips
- 1 tsp turmeric powder
- Peanut sauce for serving
- 3 tbsp soy sauce
- 1 tsp curry powder
- 1 tbsp honey
- 2 cloves garlic, minced

Instructions:
1. Marinate beef in soy sauce, honey, turmeric, curry powder, and garlic for at least 2 hours.
2. Skewer the beef strips.
3. Air fry at 180°C for 12 minutes, turning halfway.
4. Serve with peanut sauce.

Air Fryer Hungarian Pork Goulash

Prep time: 20 minutes Cooking Time: 20 minutes Servings: 4

Ingredients:
- 400g pork chunks
- 2 tbsp paprika
- Salt and pepper to taste
- 1 onion, chopped
- 1 tsp caraway seeds
- 2 cloves garlic, minced
- 250ml pork stock

Instructions:
1. Sauté onions and garlic until translucent, add pork and brown all sides. Mix in paprika, caraway seeds, salt, and pepper.
2. Transfer to the air fryer, add pork stock.
3. Cook at 160°C for 20 minutes.

Air Fryer Brazilian Beef Picanha

Prep time: 10 minutes Cooking Time: 12 minutes Servings: 4

Ingredients:
- 500g picanha (top sirloin cap)
- 2 tbsp coarse salt
- 1 tbsp olive oil

Instructions:
1. Rub the picanha with olive oil and then coat generously with coarse salt.
2. Air fry at 190°C for 12 minutes, turning halfway for medium-rare.
3. Let it rest for 5 minutes, then slice against the grain.

Air Fryer Lebanese Lamb Kebabs

Prep time: 30 minutes Cooking Time: 10 minutes Servings: 4

Ingredients:
- 400g minced lamb
- 1 onion, finely chopped
- 2 cloves garlic, minced
- 2 tsp ground cumin
- 1 tsp ground coriander
- Salt and pepper to taste

Instructions:
1. Mix all Ingredients together and shape into kebabs around skewers.
2. Air fry at 180°C for 10 minutes, turning once.

Air Fryer Japanese Pork Tonkatsu

Prep time: 20 minutes Cooking Time: 15 minutes Servings: 4

Ingredients:
- 4 pork loin chops, boneless
- Salt and pepper to taste
- 50g flour
- 2 eggs, beaten
- 150g panko breadcrumbs
- Tonkatsu sauce for serving

Instructions:
1. Season the pork chops with salt and pepper. Dredge in flour, dip in eggs, and coat with panko.
2. Air fry at 190°C for 15 minutes, turning halfway.
3. Serve with tonkatsu sauce.

Air Fryer Persian Lamb Koobideh

Prep time: 35 minutes Cooking Time: 12 minutes Servings: 4

Ingredients:
- 400g minced lamb
- 1 onion, grated and juice squeezed out
- 2 cloves garlic, minced
- 1 tsp turmeric
- Salt and pepper to taste

Instructions:
1. Mix all Ingredients and shape into long, flat skewers.
2. Air fry at 180°C for 12 minutes, turning once.

Air Fryer Spanish Pork Pinchos Morunos

Prep time: 25 minutes (plus marinating time) Cooking Time: 10 minutes Servings: 4

Ingredients:
- 400g pork tenderloin, cubed
- 1 tsp cumin
- Salt to taste
- 3 cloves garlic, minced
- 1/2 tsp oregano
- 1 tsp smoked paprika
- 2 tbsp olive oil

Instructions:
1. Mix all the marinade Ingredients and coat the pork cubes. Marinate for at least 2 hours.
2. Skewer the marinated pork.
3. Air fry at 180°C for 10 minutes, turning once.

Air Fryer Indian Lamb Seekh Kebabs

Prep time: 30 minutes Cooking Time: 10 minutes Servings: 4

Ingredients:
- 400g minced lamb
- 2 tsp garam masala
- Fresh coriander, chopped
- 1 onion, finely chopped
- 1 tsp turmeric
- Salt to taste
- 2 green chilies, minced
- 1 tsp red chili powder

Instructions:
1. Mix all the Ingredients and shape them around skewers.
2. Air fry at 180°C for 10 minutes, turning once.

Air Fryer Greek Beef Souvlaki

Prep time: 25 minutes (plus marinating time) Cooking Time: 10 minutes Servings: 4

Ingredients:
- 400g beef sirloin, cubed
- 2 cloves garlic, minced
- 3 tbsp olive oil
- 1 tsp dried oregano
- 2 tbsp lemon juice
- Salt and pepper to taste

Instructions:
1. Mix the marinade Ingredients and coat the beef cubes. Marinate for at least 3 hours.
2. Skewer the marinated beef.
3. Air fry at 180°C for 10 minutes, turning once.
- This Greek Beef Souvlaki is a refreshing combination of tangy and savoury, making it a Mediterranean favorite.

Air Fryer Mexican Pork Carnitas

Prep time: 20 minutes Cooking Time: 20 minutes Servings: 4

Ingredients:
- 500g pork shoulder, cut into chunks
- 1 tsp oregano
- 2 tbsp orange juice
- 1 tsp cumin
- 3 cloves garlic, minced
- 1 tsp chili powder
- Salt to taste

Instructions:
1. Season the pork with all the spices and garlic. Drizzle with orange juice.
2. Air fry at 180°C for 20 minutes until crispy on the outside.

Air Fryer Australian Lamb Chops

Prep time: 15 minutes Cooking Time: 12 minutes Servings: 4

Ingredients:
- 4 lamb chops
- 1 sprig rosemary, chopped
- 2 tbsp olive oil
- Salt and pepper to taste
- 2 cloves garlic, minced

Instructions:
1. Rub the lamb chops with olive oil, garlic, rosemary, salt, and pepper.
2. Air fry at 190°C for 12 minutes, turning once for medium-rare.

Air Fryer Korean Beef Bulgogi

Prep time: 30 minutes (plus marinating time) Cooking Time: 10 minutes Servings: 4

Ingredients:
- 400g thinly sliced beef sirloin
- 1 tbsp sesame oil
- 1 tsp ginger, minced
- 3 tbsp soy sauce
- 2 cloves garlic, minced
- 2 green onions, chopped
- 2 tbsp brown sugar
- 1 small pear, grated
- 1 tbsp toasted sesame seeds

Instructions:
1. Mix all the marinade Ingredients and marinate the beef slices for at least 3 hours.
2. Air fry at 180°C for 10 minutes, turning once.

French Beef Bourguignon Meatballs

Prep time: 15 minutes Cook time: 30 minutes Serves: 4

Ingredients:
- 500g ground beef
- 60g chopped fresh parsley
- 1/2 tsp salt
- 1 onion, finely chopped
- 120ml red wine
- 120g breadcrumbs
- 1 tbsp Worcestershire sauce
- 1/4 tsp black pepper
- 2 cloves garlic, minced
- 1 tbsp cornstarch
- 1 egg
- 2 tbsp tomato paste
- 2 tbsp olive oil
- 120ml beef broth
- 1 tbsp cold water

Instructions:
1. Preheat the Ninja Dual Zone Air Fryer to 180°C on zone 1 for 5 minutes.
2. In a large bowl, combine the ground beef, breadcrumbs, egg, parsley, Worcestershire sauce, tomato paste, salt, and black pepper. Mix well.

3. Shape the mixture into meatballs.
4. Place the meatballs on the crisper plate in zone 1 and air fry at 180°C for 10 minutes, turning halfway through.
5. While the meatballs are cooking, heat the olive oil in a saucepan over medium heat. Add the onion and garlic and cook for 2-3 minutes until softened.
6. Add the beef broth and red wine to the saucepan and bring to a simmer.
7. In a small bowl, whisk together the cornstarch and cold water. Add this mixture to the saucepan and stir until the sauce thickens.

Crispy Pork Schnitzel

Prep time: 15 minutes Cook time: 12 minutes Serves: 4

Ingredients:
- 4 pork schnitzels (about 150g each)
- 50g grated Parmesan cheese
- 1/2 tsp garlic powder
- 2 large eggs, beaten
- Vegetable oil, for frying
- 120g breadcrumbs
- 1 tsp dried parsley
- Salt and black pepper, to taste
- 60ml milk

Instructions:
1. Preheat the Ninja Dual Zone Air Fryer to 200°C on zone 1 for 5 minutes.
2. In a shallow dish, combine the breadcrumbs, grated Parmesan cheese, dried parsley, garlic powder, salt, and black pepper.
3. In a separate bowl, whisk together the beaten eggs and milk.
4. Dredge each pork schnitzel in the breadcrumb mixture, coating it thoroughly. Press the breadcrumbs onto the schnitzel to ensure a good coating.
5. Dip the coated schnitzel into the egg and milk mixture, allowing any excess to drip off.
6. Return the schnitzel to the breadcrumb mixture and coat it again, pressing the breadcrumbs onto the schnitzel to create a thick crust.
7. Place the coated pork schnitzels in zone 1 of the air fryer and drizzle them with vegetable oil.
8. Cook the schnitzels at 200°C for 12 minutes, flipping them halfway through the cooking time, or until they are golden brown and cooked through.
9. Once cooked, remove the crispy pork schnitzels from the air fryer and let them rest on a wire rack for a few minutes to allow the coating to crisp up.

Mexican Adobo Pork Belly Tacos with Pickled Red Onion

Prep time: 20 minutes Cook time: 45 minutes Serves: 4

Ingredients:
For the pork belly:
- 1 lb pork belly, cut into bite-sized cubes
- 2 tbsp vegetable oil
- 2 tbsp adobo sauce
- Salt and pepper, to taste

For the pickled red onion:
- 1 small red onion, thinly sliced
- 60ml water
- 1 tbsp sugar
- 60ml apple cider vinegar
- 1/2 tsp salt

For the tacos:
- 8 small corn tortillas
- 60ml crumbled queso fresco
- 1 avocado, diced
- 1 lime, cut into wedges

Instructions:
1. Preheat the Ninja Dual Zone Air Fryer to 180°C on zone 1 for 5 minutes.
2. In a bowl, toss the pork belly cubes with the adobo sauce, vegetable oil, salt, and pepper until evenly coated.
3. Arrange the pork belly cubes on the crisper plate in zone 1 and air fry at 180°C for 15-20 minutes, until the pork is crispy and browned on the outside and cooked through on the inside.
4. While the pork is cooking, make the pickled red onion: In a small bowl, whisk together the apple cider vinegar, water, sugar, and salt until the sugar and salt have dissolved. Add the sliced red onion and toss to coat. Let sit for at least 10 minutes, stirring occasionally.
5. Warm the tortillas according to package Instructions.
6. Assemble the tacos: Fill each tortilla with pork belly, pickled red onion, diced avocado, and crumbled queso fresco. Squeeze a wedge of lime over each taco and serve immediately.

Chinese Five Spice Pork Tenderloin

Prep time: 10 minutes Cook time: 15 minutes Serves: 4

Ingredients:
- 600g pork tenderloin
- 2 tbsp hoisin sauce
- 1 tsp Chinese five spice powder
- 2 cloves garlic, minced
- Salt and black pepper, to taste
- 2 tbsp soy sauce
- 1 tbsp honey
- 1 tsp grated ginger
- 1 tbsp vegetable oil
- Fresh cilantro, chopped (for garnish)

Instructions:
1. Preheat the Ninja Dual Zone Air Fryer to 200°C on zone 1 for 5 minutes.
2. In a bowl, whisk together the soy sauce, hoisin sauce, honey, Chinese five spice powder, grated ginger, minced garlic, vegetable oil, salt, and black pepper to make a marinade.
3. Place the pork tenderloin in a shallow dish and pour the marinade over it. Ensure the tenderloin is evenly coated with the marinade. Let it marinate for 10 minutes.
4. Remove the pork tenderloin from the marinade, allowing any excess marinade to drip off.
5. Place the tenderloin in zone 1 of the air fryer and cook at 200°C for 15 minutes, or until the internal temperature reaches 63°C.
6. Once cooked, remove the pork tenderloin from the air fryer and let it rest for a few minutes.
7. Slice the pork tenderloin into medallions and garnish with freshly chopped cilantro.

Chapter 5 Fish and seafood

Air-Fried Herb-Crusted Salmon

Prep time: 10 minutes   Cooking Time: 15 minutes   Servings: 2

Ingredients:
- 2 salmon fillets (150g each)
- 2 tbsp fresh parsley, chopped
- Salt and pepper to taste
- 2 tbsp olive oil
- 1 tbsp fresh dill, chopped
- 1 lemon, zested and juiced
- 50g breadcrumbs
- 1 garlic clove, minced

Instructions:
1. Mix breadcrumbs, parsley, dill, garlic, lemon zest, salt, and pepper in a bowl.
2. Brush salmon fillets with olive oil and press the breadcrumb mixture onto the top of each fillet.
3. Preheat the air fryer to 180°C.
4. Place the salmon in the air fryer and cook for 12-15 minutes or until cooked through.
5. Drizzle with fresh lemon juice before serving.

Spicy Prawn Tacos with Mango Salsa

Prep time: 15 minutes   Cooking Time: 8 minutes   Servings: 2 (2 tacos each)

Ingredients:
- 200g large prawns, peeled and deveined
- 1 tbsp paprika
- 2 tbsp olive oil
- 1 ripe mango, diced
- 1 jalapeño, seeded and finely chopped
- 1 lime, juiced
- 1 tsp cumin
- 4 small tortillas
- 50g red onion, finely chopped
- Salt to taste
- 1 tbsp chilli powder
- Salt to taste
- Mango Salsa:
- 2 tbsp fresh cilantro, chopped

Instructions:
1. Toss prawns with chilli powder, paprika, cumin, salt, and olive oil.
2. Preheat the air fryer to 180°C.
3. Cook the prawns in the air fryer for 6-8 minutes or until pink and cooked through.
4. For the mango salsa, combine all Ingredients in a bowl and mix well.
5. Serve prawns in tortillas topped with mango salsa.

Coconut-Crusted Tilapia with Pineapple Chutney

Prep time: 15 minutes   Cooking Time: 14 minutes   Servings: 2

Ingredients:
- 2 tilapia fillets (150g each)
- 2 eggs, beaten
- **Pineapple Chutney:**
- 100g pineapple, diced
- 1 tbsp apple cider vinegar
- 100g shredded coconut
- Salt and pepper to taste

- 2 tbsp brown sugar
- 1 red chilli, finely chopped

Instructions:
1. Season tilapia fillets with salt and pepper.
2. Dip each fillet into beaten eggs, then coat with shredded coconut.
3. Preheat the air fryer to 180°C.
4. Cook the tilapia in the air fryer for 12-14 minutes or until golden brown.
5. For the pineapple chutney, combine all Ingredients in a saucepan and simmer for 10 minutes.
6. Serve tilapia with chutney on the side.

Crispy Calamari Rings with Aioli Dip

Prep time: 20 minutes   Cooking Time: 10 minutes   Servings: 2-3

Ingredients:
- 200g calamari rings
- Salt and pepper to taste
- **Aioli Dip:**
- 100ml mayonnaise
- 1 tsp lemon zest
- 100g flour
- 2 eggs, beaten
- 2 garlic cloves, minced
- 1 tsp paprika
- 150g breadcrumbs
- 1 tbsp lemon juice

Instructions:
1. Season flour with paprika, salt, and pepper.
2. Dip each calamari ring into flour, then into beaten eggs, and finally coat with breadcrumbs.
3. Preheat the air fryer to 190°C.
4. Cook the calamari rings in batches for 8-10 minutes or until golden and crispy.
5. For the aioli dip, mix all Ingredients in a bowl.
6. Serve calamari hot with aioli dip.

Lemon-Herb Haddock with Asparagus

Prep time: 15 minutes (including marination)   Cooking Time: 15 minutes   Servings: 2

Ingredients:
- 2 haddock fillets (150g each)
- 1 lemon, zested and juiced
- Salt and pepper to taste
- 2 tbsp olive oil
- 2 tbsp fresh parsley, chopped
- 200g asparagus spears, trimmed

Instructions:
1. Mix olive oil, lemon zest, lemon juice, parsley, salt, and pepper in a bowl.
2. Coat haddock fillets with the marinade and let sit for 10 minutes.
3. Preheat the air fryer to 180°C.
4. Place the haddock and asparagus in the air fryer. Cook for 12-15 minutes or until the fish is flaky and asparagus is tender.
5. Serve immediately.

Spiced Mussels with Tomato Sauce

Prep time: 15 minutes   Cooking Time: 12 minutes   Servings: 2-3

Ingredients:
- 500g mussels, cleaned and debearded
- 2 tbsp olive oil
- 1 onion, finely chopped

- 2 garlic cloves, minced
- 1 tsp chilli flakes
- 200ml tomato sauce
- Salt to taste
- 1 tsp smoked paprika
- 2 tbsp fresh coriander, chopped

Instructions:
1. Heat olive oil in a pan. Add onions and garlic and sauté until translucent.
2. Add tomato sauce, smoked paprika, chilli flakes, and salt. Cook for 5 minutes.
3. Add mussels to the sauce and mix well.
4. Transfer the mixture to a suitable air fryer dish.
5. Cook in the air fryer at 180°C for 10-12 minutes or until mussels open up.
6. Garnish with fresh coriander before serving.

Thai-Inspired Fish Cakes with Sweet Chili Sauce

Prep time: 20 minutes   Cooking Time: 12 minutes   Servings: 2-3

Ingredients:
- 300g white fish fillets, boneless
- 2 tbsp Thai red curry paste
- 1 egg
- 1 tbsp fish sauce
- 1 tsp sugar
- 50g green beans, finely chopped
- 2 kaffir lime leaves, finely sliced
- Fresh coriander for garnish
- Sweet Chili Sauce (store-bought or homemade)

Instructions:
1. Blend fish fillets, curry paste, egg, fish sauce, and sugar in a food processor until smooth.
2. Transfer to a bowl and mix in green beans and kaffir lime leaves.
3. Shape the mixture into small patties.
4. Preheat the air fryer to 190°C.
5. Cook the fish cakes for 10-12 minutes or until golden and cooked through.
6. Serve with sweet chilli sauce and garnish with fresh coriander.

Moroccan Spiced Shrimp with Couscous

Prep time: 15 minutes   Cooking Time: 8 minutes   Servings: 2

Ingredients:
- 200g large shrimp, peeled and deveined
- 1 tbsp olive oil
- 1 tsp ground cumin
- 1 tsp ground coriander
- 1 tsp paprika
- Salt to taste
- 150g couscous
- 300ml hot vegetable broth
- Fresh parsley, chopped for garnish

Instructions:
1. Toss shrimp with olive oil, cumin, coriander, paprika, and salt.
2. Preheat the air fryer to 190°C.
3. Cook the shrimp in the air fryer for 6-8 minutes or until pink and cooked through.
4. Meanwhile, pour hot vegetable broth over couscous in a bowl. Cover and let sit for 5 minutes. Fluff with a fork.
5. Serve shrimp over couscous and garnish with fresh parsley.

Brazilian Coconut Fish Stew (Moqueca)

Prep time: 15 minutes   Cooking Time: 18 minutes   Servings: 2

Ingredients:
- 300g firm white fish fillets, cut into chunks
- 1 red bell pepper, sliced
- 2 tbsp lime juice
- 1 onion, sliced
- 2 garlic cloves, minced
- 2 tbsp fresh cilantro, chopped
- 1 tbsp olive oil
- 200ml coconut milk
- Salt and pepper to taste

Instructions:
1. In a pan, heat olive oil and sauté onions, bell pepper, and garlic until soft.
2. Add fish chunks, coconut milk, lime juice, salt, and pepper.
3. Transfer the mixture to a suitable air fryer dish.
4. Cook in the air fryer at 180°C for 15-18 minutes or until the fish is cooked through.
5. Garnish with fresh cilantro before serving.

Japanese Teriyaki Glazed Eel (Unagi)

Prep time: 15 minutes Cooking Time: 12 minutes Servings: 2

Ingredients:
- 200g fresh eel fillets
- 2 tbsp sake
- White sesame seeds for garnish
- 3 tbsp soy sauce
- 1 tbsp sugar
- 2 tbsp mirin
- 1 tsp grated ginger

Instructions:
1. In a saucepan, combine soy sauce, mirin, sake, sugar, and ginger. Simmer until the sauce thickens slightly.
2. Coat eel fillets with the teriyaki sauce.
3. Preheat the air fryer to 190°C.
4. Cook the eel in the air fryer for 10-12 minutes or until cooked through, brushing with extra sauce halfway.
5. Garnish with white sesame seeds before serving.

Greek Octopus with Lemon and Oregano

Prep time: 10 minutes Cooking Time: 10 minutes Servings: 2

Ingredients:
- 300g baby octopus, cleaned
- Zest and juice of 1 lemon
- 2 tbsp olive oil
- 2 tbsp fresh oregano, chopped
- 2 garlic cloves, minced
- Salt and pepper to taste

Instructions:
1. Toss baby octopus with olive oil, garlic, lemon zest, lemon juice, oregano, salt, and pepper.
2. Preheat the air fryer to 180°C.
3. Cook the octopus in the air fryer for 8-10 minutes or until tender and slightly crispy.
4. Serve immediately.

Vietnamese Lemongrass Clams

Prep time: 15 minutes Cooking Time: 10 minutes Servings: 2-3

Ingredients:
- 500g fresh clams, cleaned
- 1 stalk lemongrass, finely chopped

- 3 garlic cloves, minced
- 1 tsp sugar
- 2 red chilies, sliced
- Fresh cilantro for garnish
- 2 tbsp fish sauce

Instructions:
1. In a bowl, mix lemongrass, garlic, chilies, fish sauce, and sugar.
2. Toss clams in the mixture, ensuring they are well coated.
3. Transfer the clams to a suitable air fryer dish.
4. Cook in the air fryer at 180°C for 8-10 minutes or until clams open up.
5. Discard any unopened clams and garnish with fresh cilantro before serving.

Peruvian Ceviche Tostadas

Prep time: 20 minutes   Cooking Time: 5 minutes   Servings: 2

Ingredients:
- 200g fresh white fish, diced (like sea bass or snapper)
- 1 red onion, thinly sliced
- Salt to taste
- 1 red chilli, finely chopped
- 4 small tortillas
- Juice of 3 limes
- 2 tbsp fresh cilantro, chopped

Instructions:
1. Combine fish, lime juice, red onion, chilli, and cilantro in a bowl. Season with salt and let it marinate for 15 minutes.
2. Preheat the air fryer to 190°C.
3. Cook the tortillas in the air fryer for 3-5 minutes or until crispy.
4. Top each crispy tortilla with ceviche mixture.

Swedish Dill and Lemon Butter Shrimp

Prep time: 10 minutes   Cooking Time: 8 minutes   Servings: 2

Ingredients:
- 250g large shrimp, peeled and deveined
- Zest and juice of 1 lemon
- Salt and pepper to taste
- 50g butter, melted
- 3 tbsp fresh dill, chopped

Instructions:
1. Mix melted butter, lemon zest, lemon juice, dill, salt, and pepper in a bowl.
2. Toss shrimp in the mixture.
3. Preheat the air fryer to 190°C.
4. Cook the shrimp in the air fryer for 6-8 minutes or until pink and cooked through.
5. Drizzle with any remaining butter mixture before serving.

Indian Tandoori Lobster Tails

Prep time: 40 minutes (including marination)   Cooking Time: 12 minutes   Servings: 2

Ingredients:
- 2 lobster tails, split in half
- 2 tbsp tandoori masala
- 2 garlic cloves, minced
- 100ml yoghourt
- 1 tsp turmeric powder
- 1 tbsp ginger, grated
- 2 tbsp lemon juice
- 1 tsp red chilli powder
- Salt to taste

- Fresh coriander for garnish

Instructions:
1. Mix yoghurt, lemon juice, tandoori masala, turmeric, chilli powder, garlic, ginger, and salt in a bowl.
2. Coat the lobster tails in the marinade and let sit for at least 30 minutes.
3. Preheat the air fryer to 190°C.
4. Cook the lobster tails in the air fryer for 10-12 minutes or until the meat is opaque and cooked through.
5. Garnish with fresh coriander before serving.

Peruvian Ceviche Tostadas

Prep time: 20 minutes   Cooking Time: 5 minutes   Servings: 2

Ingredients:
- 200g fresh white fish, diced (like sea bass or snapper)
- 1 red onion, thinly sliced
- Salt to taste
- 1 red chilli, finely chopped
- 4 small tortillas
- Juice of 3 limes
- 2 tbsp fresh cilantro, chopped

Instructions:
1. Combine fish, lime juice, red onion, chilli, and cilantro in a bowl. Season with salt and let it marinate for 15 minutes.
2. Preheat the air fryer to 190°C.
3. Cook the tortillas in the air fryer for 3-5 minutes or until crispy.
4. Top each crispy tortilla with ceviche mixture.

Swedish Dill and Lemon Butter Shrimp

Prep time: 10 minutes   Cooking Time: 8 minutes   Servings: 2

Ingredients:
- 250g large shrimp, peeled and deveined
- Zest and juice of 1 lemon
- Salt and pepper to taste
- 50g butter, melted
- 3 tbsp fresh dill, chopped

Instructions:
1. Mix melted butter, lemon zest, lemon juice, dill, salt, and pepper in a bowl.
2. Toss shrimp in the mixture.
3. Preheat the air fryer to 190°C.
4. Cook the shrimp in the air fryer for 6-8 minutes or until pink and cooked through.
5. Drizzle with any remaining butter mixture before serving.

Indian Tandoori Lobster Tails

Prep time: 40 minutes (including marination)   Cooking Time: 12 minutes   Servings: 2

Ingredients:
- 2 lobster tails, split in half
- 2 tbsp tandoori masala
- 100ml yoghourt
- 1 tsp turmeric powder
- 2 tbsp lemon juice
- 1 tsp red chilli powder

- 2 garlic cloves, minced
- 1 tbsp ginger, grated
- Salt to taste
- Fresh coriander for garnish

Instructions:
1. Mix yoghourt, lemon juice, tandoori masala, turmeric, chilli powder, garlic, ginger, and salt in a bowl.
2. Coat the lobster tails in the marinade and let sit for at least 30 minutes.
3. Preheat the air fryer to 190°C.
4. Cook the lobster tails in the air fryer for 10-12 minutes or until the meat is opaque and cooked through.
5. Garnish with fresh coriander before serving.

Italian Seafood Risotto Arancini

Prep time: 15 minutes   Cooking Time: 12 minutes   Servings: 2-3

Ingredients:
- 300g leftover seafood risotto (pre-cooked with mixed seafood)
- 100g mozzarella cheese, cut into small cubes
- 150g breadcrumbs
- 2 eggs, beaten
- Olive oil for brushing

Instructions:
1. Take a spoonful of risotto and flatten it in your hand. Place a cube of mozzarella in the centre and shape the risotto around it to form a ball.
2. Dip each ball into beaten eggs, then coat with breadcrumbs.
3. Preheat the air fryer to 190°C.
4. Place the arancini in the air fryer and brush lightly with olive oil.
5. Cook for 10-12 minutes or until golden brown.

Filipino Garlic Pepper Squid

Prep time: 10 minutes   Cooking Time: 7 minutes   Servings: 2

Ingredients:
- 250g squid rings
- 50ml soy sauce
- 3 garlic cloves, minced
- 1 tsp black pepper, freshly ground
- 2 green onions, chopped

Instructions:
1. Mix soy sauce, garlic, and black pepper in a bowl.
2. Toss squid rings in the mixture.
3. Preheat the air fryer to 190°C.
4. Cook the squid in the air fryer for 5-7 minutes or until tender.
5. Garnish with chopped green onions before serving.

Cajun Shrimp and Grits

Prep time: 10 minutes   Cook time: 20 minutes   Serves: 4

Ingredients:
For the shrimp:
- 400g large shrimp, peeled and deveined
- 2 tbsp Cajun seasoning

- 2 tbsp olive oil
- Salt and black pepper, to taste

For the grits:
- 200g quick-cooking grits
- 750ml water
- 60ml whole milk
- 30g unsalted butter
- Salt, to taste

For serving:
- 2 spring onions, thinly sliced
- Fresh parsley, chopped

Instructions:

1. Preheat the Ninja Dual Zone Air Fryer to 200°C on zone 1 for 5 minutes.
2. In a bowl, toss the peeled and deveined shrimp with Cajun seasoning, olive oil, salt, and black pepper until well coated.
3. Place the seasoned shrimp in zone 1 of the air fryer and airfryer at 200°C for 6-8 minutes, or until the shrimp are pink and cooked through.
4. While the shrimp are cooking, prepare the grits. In a saucepan, bring the water to a boil. Stir in the quick-cooking grits and reduce the heat to low. Cook the grits according to the package Instructions, usually for about 5 minutes, stirring occasionally.
5. Once the grits are cooked, stir in the whole milk, unsalted butter, and salt to taste. Continue cooking for another 2-3 minutes until the grits are creamy and smooth.
6. Divide the cooked grits among 4 serving bowls.
7. Remove the cooked shrimp from the air fryer and place them on top of the grits.
8. Garnish with sliced spring onions and chopped parsley.
9. Serve the Cajun shrimp and grits hot, and enjoy the delightful combination of flavours and textures.

Cajun Blackened Salmon

Prep time: 5 mins Cook Time: 8 minutes Servings: 2

Ingredients:

- 300 grams salmon fillets
- Paprika
- Dried thyme
- Oregano
- Garlic powder
- Onion powder
- Cayenne pepper (adjust to taste)
- Salt
- Black pepper
- 30 ml olive oil

Instructions:

1. Preheat your Ninja Dual Zone Air Fryer to 200C. This will help get that char on the salmon.
2. In a small bowl, combine the paprika, dried thyme, oregano, garlic powder, onion powder, cayenne pepper, salt, and black pepper to create the Cajun spice blend.
3. Brush both sides of the salmon fillets with olive oil to prevent sticking.
4. Sprinkle the Cajun spice blend generously over both sides of the salmon fillets, pressing it gently so it sticks.
5. Carefully place the seasoned salmon fillets on the non stick plates and into the Air Fryer drawers, skin-side down if they have skin.
6. Cook the salmon for about 3-4 minutes per side, depending on the thickness of the fillets, until the fish is opaque and flakes easily with a fork. The spices should create a dark, flavorful crust on the fish.
7. Once cooked, transfer the Cajun blackened salmon fillets to a serving platter.
8. Serve the salmon hot with a squeeze of fresh lemon juice and garnish with chopped parsley or cilantro, if you would prefer.

Chapter 6 Vegetable and Vegetarian

Air Fryer Italian Vegan Eggplant Parmesan

Prep time: 20 minutes Cooking Time: 25 minutes Servings: 4

Ingredients:
- 2 large eggplants, sliced
- 400g canned tomatoes, crushed
- 3 cloves garlic, minced
- 200g vegan mozzarella cheese, shredded
- 100g breadcrumbs
- 1 tbsp olive oil
- 2 tsp dried basil
- Salt and pepper to taste

Instructions:
1. Dredge eggplant slices in breadcrumbs.
2. Air fry eggplant slices at 190°C for 15 minutes or until golden.
3. In a pan, sauté garlic in olive oil. Add crushed tomatoes, basil, salt, and pepper. Simmer for 10 minutes.
4. In an air fryer-safe dish, layer eggplant slices, tomato sauce, and vegan cheese.
5. Air fry at 180°C for 10 minutes or until the cheese melts.

Air Fryer Middle Eastern Falafel Bowl

Prep time: 30 minutes (plus soaking time) Cooking Time: 20 minutes Servings: 4

Ingredients:
- 300g dried chickpeas, soaked overnight
- 1 onion, chopped
- 3 cloves garlic
- 2 tsp ground cumin
- 1 tsp ground coriander
- 1 handful fresh parsley
- Salt to taste
- 50g tahini
- 1 lemon, juiced
- Fresh vegetables for serving (lettuce, tomatoes, cucumbers)

Instructions:
1. In a food processor, combine soaked chickpeas, onion, garlic, spices, parsley, and salt. Process until smooth.
2. Shape the mixture into balls and air fry at 190°C for 20 minutes or until golden.
3. Mix tahini and lemon juice for the sauce.
4. Serve falafel with fresh vegetables and drizzle with tahini sauce.

Air Fryer Indian Vegetable Samosas

Prep time: 40 minutes Cooking Time: 20 minutes Servings: 4

Ingredients:
- 200g all-purpose flour
- 50g vegetable oil
- 100ml water
- 2 potatoes, boiled and mashed
- 100g green peas
- 1 onion, chopped
- 2 tsp ground cumin
- 2 tsp garam masala
- Salt to taste

Instructions:
1. Mix flour, 30g oil, and water to form a dough. Rest for 30 minutes.
2. In a pan, sauté onions in remaining oil. Add spices, potatoes, and peas. Mix well.

3. Roll out the dough and cut into circles. Fill with vegetable mixture and shape into triangles.
4. Air fry samosas at 190°C for 20 minutes or until golden.

Air Fryer Thai Vegan Pineapple Fried Rice

Prep time: 15 minutes Cooking Time: 25 minutes Servings: 4

Ingredients:
- 400g cooked jasmine rice
- 50g roasted cashews
- 3 green onions, sliced
- 200g pineapple chunks
- 2 tbsp soy sauce
- 1 tsp curry powder
- 100g bell peppers, sliced
- 2 tbsp vegetable oil
- Fresh cilantro for garnish

Instructions:
1. In a pan, heat oil and sauté bell peppers.
2. Add rice, pineapple, soy sauce, and curry powder. Mix well.
3. Transfer to an air fryer-safe dish and air fry at 180°C for 25 minutes.
4. Garnish with roasted cashews, green onions, and cilantro.

Air Fryer Mexican Vegan Stuffed Peppers

Prep time: 20 minutes Cooking Time: 30 minutes Servings: 4

Ingredients:
- 4 bell peppers, tops removed
- 150g corn kernels
- 2 tsp ground cumin
- 2 tbsp vegetable oil
- 200g cooked rice
- 1 onion, chopped
- 1 tsp smoked paprika
- Salt and pepper to taste
- 150g black beans
- 2 cloves garlic, minced
- 200g tomato salsa

Instructions:
1. In a pan, heat oil and sauté onions and garlic.
2. Add rice, beans, corn, spices, and salsa. Mix well.
3. Stuff the bell peppers with the mixture.
4. Air fry stuffed peppers at 180°C for 30 minutes or until peppers are tender.

Air Fryer Moroccan Vegan Tagine

Prep time: 20 minutes Cooking Time: 35 minutes Servings: 4

Ingredients:
- 2 zucchinis, sliced
- 400g canned tomatoes, crushed
- 3 cloves garlic, minced
- 1 tsp ground cinnamon
- Salt and pepper to taste
- 2 carrots, sliced
- 2 tsp ground cumin
- 2 tbsp olive oil
- 200g chickpeas, cooked
- 1 onion, chopped
- 2 tsp paprika
- Fresh cilantro, chopped

Instructions:
1. In a pan, heat oil and sauté onions and garlic until translucent.
2. Add spices, tomatoes, chickpeas, zucchinis, and carrots.
3. Transfer the mixture to an air fryer-safe dish.
4. Air fry at 180°C for 35 minutes.

5. Garnish with fresh cilantro before serving.

Air Fryer Japanese Vegan Tempura Vegetables

Prep time: 25 minutes · Cooking Time: 15 minutes · Servings: 4

Ingredients:
- Assorted vegetables (bell peppers, zucchinis, mushrooms)
- 120g all-purpose flour
- 150ml sparkling water, cold
- 1 tsp soy sauce
- Salt to taste
- Dipping sauce for serving

Instructions:
1. Slice the vegetables into bite-sized pieces.
2. Mix flour, cold sparkling water, soy sauce, and salt to form a smooth batter.
3. Dip each vegetable slice into the batter, ensuring it's fully coated.
4. Air fry at 190°C for 15 minutes, or until golden brown.
5. Serve with your favourite dipping sauce.

Air Fryer French Ratatouille

Prep time: 20 minutes · Cooking Time: 40 minutes · Servings: 4

Ingredients:
- 1 eggplant, diced
- 1 zucchini, diced
- 1 bell pepper, diced
- 400g canned tomatoes, crushed
- 1 onion, chopped
- 3 cloves garlic, minced
- 2 tbsp olive oil
- 1 tsp dried basil
- 1 tsp dried thyme
- Salt and pepper to taste

Instructions:
1. In a pan, heat oil and sauté onions and garlic until fragrant.
2. Add all vegetables and canned tomatoes to the pan.
3. Season with basil, thyme, salt, and pepper.
4. Transfer the mixture to an air fryer-safe dish.
5. Air fry at 180°C for 40 minutes, stirring occasionally.

Air Fryer Mexican Vegan Tofu Tacos

Prep time: 30 minutes · Cooking Time: 20 minutes · Servings: 4

Ingredients:
- 300g firm tofu, crumbled
- 4 vegan taco shells
- 1 onion, chopped
- 2 cloves garlic, minced
- 2 tsp smoked paprika
- 1 tsp ground cumin
- 2 tbsp olive oil
- Fresh salsa and lettuce for serving

Instructions:
1. In a pan, heat oil and sauté onions and garlic until translucent.
2. Add crumbled tofu, paprika, and cumin. Cook until tofu is golden and crispy.
3. Air fry taco shells at 180°C for 5 minutes, or until crispy.
4. Fill each taco with tofu mixture, top with fresh salsa and lettuce.

Air Fryer Indonesian Vegan Gado-Gado

Prep time: 25 minutes Cooking Time: 15 minutes Servings: 4

Ingredients:
- Assorted blanched vegetables (green beans, bean sprouts, cabbage)
- 200g tofu, cubed
- 100g roasted peanuts
- 1 clove garlic
- 1 tsp tamarind paste
- 1 tsp soy sauce
- 1 red chilli
- Salt and sugar to taste
- 150ml water

Instructions:
1. Air fry tofu cubes at 190°C for 15 minutes, or until golden.
2. Blend roasted peanuts, garlic, tamarind paste, soy sauce, chilli, salt, sugar, and water to form a smooth sauce.
3. Arrange blanched vegetables on a plate, top with tofu cubes, and drizzle with the peanut sauce.

Air Fryer African Vegan Bobotie

Prep time: 30 minutes Cooking Time: 40 minutes Servings: 4

Ingredients:
- 200g lentils, cooked
- 1 onion, chopped
- 2 cloves garlic, minced
- 2 tbsp curry powder
- 1 tbsp turmeric
- 150g breadcrumbs
- 400g canned tomatoes, crushed
- 2 tbsp apple cider vinegar
- 100ml coconut milk
- 1 tbsp olive oil
- Salt and pepper to taste

Instructions:
1. In a pan, sauté onions and garlic in olive oil until translucent.
2. Add curry powder, turmeric, lentils, and tomatoes. Cook for 10 minutes.
3. Stir in vinegar, breadcrumbs, and half the coconut milk. Season with salt and pepper.
4. Transfer the mixture to an air fryer-safe dish.
5. Whisk the remaining coconut milk and pour over the lentil mixture.
6. Air fry at 180°C for 40 minutes.

Air Fryer Caribbean Vegan Jackfruit "Pulled Pork"

Prep time: 20 minutes Cooking Time: 30 minutes Servings: 4

Ingredients:
- 400g canned jackfruit, drained and shredded
- 1 onion, chopped
- 2 cloves garlic, minced
- 3 tbsp barbecue sauce
- 2 tsp smoked paprika
- 1 tsp cayenne pepper
- 1 tbsp olive oil
- Salt to taste

Instructions:
1. In a pan, heat oil and sauté onions and garlic.
2. Add shredded jackfruit, smoked paprika, cayenne, and barbecue sauce.
3. Cook for 15 minutes, allowing flavours to meld.
4. Transfer to an air fryer-safe dish and air fry at 180°C for 30 minutes.

Air Fryer Spanish Vegan Paella

Prep time: 25 minutes Cooking Time: 40 minutes Servings: 4

Ingredients:
- 200g Arborio rice
- 1 green bell pepper, sliced
- 1 onion, chopped
- 400ml vegetable broth
- 2 tbsp olive oil
- 1 red bell pepper, sliced
- 100g green beans, chopped
- 3 cloves garlic, minced
- A pinch of saffron threads
- Salt and pepper to taste

Instructions:
1. In a pan, heat oil and sauté onions, garlic, and bell peppers.
2. Add rice and stir for a few minutes.
3. Pour in vegetable broth infused with saffron. Season with salt and pepper.
4. Transfer the mixture to an air fryer-safe dish.
5. Air fry at 180°C for 40 minutes or until rice is cooked.

Air Fryer Mediterranean Vegan Stuffed Tomatoes

Prep time: 20 minutes Cooking Time: 30 minutes Servings: 4

Ingredients:
- 4 large tomatoes, tops cut and hollowed out
- 1 zucchini, chopped
- 2 cloves garlic, minced
- 2 tbsp olive oil
- Salt and pepper to taste
- 150g cooked quinoa
- 1 onion, chopped
- 50g black olives, sliced
- 2 tsp dried oregano

Instructions:
1. In a pan, heat oil and sauté onions, garlic, and zucchini.
2. Mix in cooked quinoa, olives, oregano, salt, and pepper.
3. Stuff each tomato with the quinoa mixture.
4. Air fry stuffed tomatoes at 180°C for 30 minutes.

Air Fryer British Vegan Shepherd's Pie

Prep time: 30 minutes Cooking Time: 45 minutes Servings: 4

Ingredients:
- 200g lentils, cooked
- 1 onion, chopped
- 400g canned tomatoes, crushed
- 400g potatoes, boiled and mashed with a splash of almond milk
- 2 tbsp olive oil
- 1 tsp dried thyme
- 2 carrots, chopped
- 3 cloves garlic, minced
- 1 tsp dried rosemary
- Salt and pepper to taste

Instructions:
1. In a pan, heat oil and sauté onions, garlic, and carrots until softened.
2. Add lentils, crushed tomatoes, rosemary, thyme, salt, and pepper. Cook for 10 minutes.

3. Transfer the lentil mixture to an air fryer-safe dish and spread evenly.
4. Top with the mashed potatoes, creating a smooth layer.
5. Air fry at 180°C for 45 minutes or until the top is golden brown.

Air Fryer Greek Vegan Moussaka

Prep time: 40 minutes   Cooking Time: 50 minutes   Servings: 4

Ingredients:
- 2 large eggplants, sliced
- 400g canned tomatoes, crushed
- 3 cloves garlic, minced
- 1 tsp ground cinnamon
- 200ml unsweetened almond milk
- 2 tbsp vegan butter
- 200g lentils, cooked
- 1 onion, chopped
- 2 tbsp olive oil
- 1 tsp dried oregano
- 2 tbsp all-purpose flour
- Salt and pepper to taste

Instructions:
1. Air fry eggplant slices at 190°C for 10 minutes, set aside.
2. In a pan, heat oil and sauté onions and garlic. Add lentils, tomatoes, cinnamon, and oregano.
3. For the béchamel, melt vegan butter in a pan, whisk in flour, then gradually add almond milk. Cook until thickened.
4. In an air fryer-safe dish, layer eggplant slices, lentil mixture, and béchamel.
5. Air fry at 180°C for 50 minutes or until golden brown.

Air Fryer Peruvian Vegan Quinoa Stuffed Peppers

Prep time: 25 minutes   Cooking Time: 35 minutes   Servings: 4

Ingredients:
- 4 bell peppers, tops removed
- 100g corn kernels
- 2 cloves garlic, minced
- 1 tsp ground cumin
- Salt and pepper to taste
- 200g quinoa, cooked
- 1 onion, chopped
- 2 tbsp olive oil
- 1 tsp smoked paprika

Instructions:
1. In a pan, heat oil and sauté onions and garlic until translucent.
2. Add corn, cumin, smoked paprika, salt, and cooked quinoa. Mix well.
3. Stuff each bell pepper with the quinoa mixture.
4. Air fry stuffed peppers at 180°C for 35 minutes or until peppers are tender.

Air Fryer Vietnamese Vegan Spring Rolls

Prep time: 30 minutes   Cooking Time: 15 minutes   Servings: 4

Ingredients:
- Rice paper sheets (8 pieces)
- 1 carrot, julienned
- Fresh mint leaves
- 100g vermicelli noodles, cooked
- 1 cucumber, julienned
- 2 tbsp soy sauce

- 1 tbsp lime juice
- 1 tsp chilli flakes

Instructions:
1. Wet rice paper sheets briefly and lay flat.
2. Place a small amount of vermicelli noodles, carrot, cucumber, and mint in the centre.
3. Roll tightly, tucking in the sides.
4. Air fry the rolls at 190°C for 15 minutes, or until crispy.
5. Mix soy sauce, lime juice, and chilli flakes for the dipping sauce.

Air Fryer Middle Eastern Vegan Falafel Wraps

Prep time: 30 minutes (plus soaking)　　Cooking Time: 20 minutes　　Servings: 4

Ingredients:
- 200g dried chickpeas, soaked overnight
- 3 cloves garlic, minced
- 2 tsp ground coriander
- 4 vegan wraps
- Fresh lettuce, tomatoes, and cucumber for serving
- 1 tbsp lemon juice
- 1 onion, chopped
- 2 tsp ground cumin
- A handful of fresh parsley, chopped
- 3 tbsp tahini
- Salt and pepper to taste

Instructions:
1. Blend soaked chickpeas, onion, garlic, cumin, coriander, parsley, salt, and pepper in a food processor until a coarse mixture forms.
2. Shape into small patties and air fry at 190°C for 20 minutes or until golden brown.
3. Mix tahini with lemon juice to make the sauce.
4. Serve falafels in wraps with fresh veggies and drizzle with tahini sauce.

Air Fryer Italian Vegan Eggplant Parmesan

Prep time: 30 minutes　　Cooking Time: 40 minutes　　Servings: 4

Ingredients:
- 2 large eggplants, sliced
- 1 onion, chopped
- 200g vegan mozzarella cheese, shredded
- 1 tsp dried oregano
- Salt and pepper to taste
- 400g canned tomatoes, crushed
- 3 cloves garlic, minced
- 2 tbsp olive oil
- 1 tsp dried basil

Instructions:
1. Air fry eggplant slices at 190°C for 10 minutes or until slightly golden.
2. In a pan, sauté onions and garlic in olive oil. Add crushed tomatoes, oregano, basil, salt, and pepper. Cook for 10 minutes.
3. In an air fryer-safe dish, layer eggplant slices, tomato sauce, and vegan cheese.
4. Air fry at 180°C for 40 minutes or until bubbly and golden.

Indian Spiced Okra

Prep time: 10 minutes　　Cook time: 15 minutes　　Serves: 4

Ingredients:

- 500g okra, washed and dried
- 1 tsp coriander seeds
- 1/2 tsp red chilli powder
- 2 tbsp vegetable oil
- 1/2 tsp turmeric powder
- Salt, to taste
- 1 tsp cumin seeds

Instructions:

1. Preheat the Ninja Dual Zone Air Fryer to 200°C on zone 1 for 5 minutes.
2. Trim the ends of the okra and cut them into 1-inch pieces.
3. In a bowl, mix together the vegetable oil, cumin seeds, coriander seeds, turmeric powder, red chilli powder, and salt.
4. Add the okra pieces to the bowl and toss them with the spice mixture.
5. Place the okra in zone 2 of the air fryer and air fry at 200°C for 15 minutes, shaking the basket halfway through the cooking time.
6. Once the okra is crispy and cooked through, remove from the air fryer and serve immediately.

Cauliflower "Steak"

Prep time: 10 minutes   Cook time: 20 minutes   Serves: 4

Ingredients:

- 1 large cauliflower head, sliced into thick "steaks"
- 2 cloves garlic, minced
- 1/2 tsp dried thyme
- 2 tbsp olive oil
- 1 tsp smoked paprika
- Salt and black pepper, to taste

Instructions:

1. Preheat the Ninja Dual Zone Air Fryer to 200°C on zone 1 for 5 minutes.
2. In a small bowl, mix together the olive oil, minced garlic, smoked paprika, dried thyme, salt, and black pepper.
3. Brush both sides of the cauliflower "steaks" with the seasoned oil mixture.
4. Place the cauliflower "steaks" in zone 1 of the air fryer.
5. Cook the cauliflower at 200°C for 20 minutes, flipping them halfway through the cooking time, or until they are tender and lightly browned.
6. Once cooked, remove the cauliflower "steaks" from the air fryer and let them cool for a few minutes before serving.

Chapter 7 Sides and appetisers

Air Fryer Greek Vegan Spanakopita Bites

Prep time: 30 minutes Cooking Time: 15 minutes Servings: 4

Ingredients:
- 300g fresh spinach, chopped
- 2 tbsp olive oil
- 2 cloves garlic, minced
- Salt to taste
- 200g vegan feta cheese, crumbled
- 1 onion, finely chopped
- Vegan phyllo pastry sheets

Instructions:
1. In a pan, heat oil and sauté onions and garlic until translucent.
2. Add spinach and cook until wilted. Remove from heat and mix in vegan feta. Season with salt.
3. Place a spoonful of filling on each phyllo sheet, fold, and brush with olive oil.
4. Air fry at 180°C for 15 minutes or until golden brown.

Air Fryer Korean Vegan Kimchi Pancakes

Prep time: 20 minutes Cooking Time: 15 minutes Servings: 4

Ingredients:
- 200g kimchi, chopped
- 2 green onions, chopped
- 100g all-purpose flour
- 1 tbsp sesame oil
- 150ml water
- Soy sauce for dipping

Instructions:
1. In a bowl, mix flour, water, kimchi, and green onions to form a batter.
2. Spoon the batter onto the air fryer tray to form pancakes.
3. Air fry at 190°C for 15 minutes, flipping halfway.
4. Serve with soy sauce.

Air Fryer Brazilian Vegan Cheese Bites (Pão de Queijo)

Prep time: 30 minutes Cooking Time: 20 minutes Servings: 4

Ingredients:
- 250g tapioca flour
- 150g vegan cheese, grated
- 150ml almond milk
- Salt to taste
- 2 tbsp olive oil

Instructions:
1. In a bowl, mix all Ingredients until a smooth dough forms.
2. Shape into small balls and place on the air fryer tray.
3. Air fry at 190°C for 20 minutes or until golden brown.

Air Fryer Moroccan Vegan Lentil Fritters

Prep time: 40 minutes (including soaking) Cooking Time: 20 minutes Servings: 4

Ingredients:
- 200g dried lentils, soaked for 2 hours
- 1 tsp ground cumin
- 1 tbsp fresh cilantro, chopped
- 1 onion, chopped
- 1 tsp ground coriander
- Salt to taste
- 2 cloves garlic, minced

Instructions:
1. Drain lentils and blend with onion, garlic, and spices until a coarse mixture forms.
2. Shape into small patties and place on the air fryer tray.
3. Air fry at 190°C for 20 minutes, flipping halfway.

Air Fryer Spanish Vegan Patatas Bravas

Prep time: 20 minutes   Cooking Time: 25 minutes   Servings: 4

Ingredients:
- 500g potatoes, diced
- 200g canned tomatoes, crushed
- 2 tbsp olive oil
- 1 tsp smoked paprika
- Salt to taste
- 1 tsp chilli powder

Instructions:
1. Toss potatoes with olive oil and salt. Air fry at 190°C for 25 minutes or until golden brown.
2. In a pan, heat crushed tomatoes with smoked paprika and chilli powder. Simmer until thickened.
3. Serve potatoes hot with the spicy sauce.

Air Fryer Chinese Vegan Spring Onion Pancakes

Prep time: 30 minutes   Cooking Time: 15 minutes   Servings: 4

Ingredients:
- 250g all-purpose flour
- 2 tbsp sesame oil
- 150ml water
- Salt to taste
- 2 spring onions, finely chopped

Instructions:
1. Mix flour and water to form a dough. Knead until smooth.
2. Roll out dough and sprinkle with spring onions and salt. Fold and roll again.
3. Cut into rounds and brush with sesame oil.
4. Air fry at 190°C for 15 minutes or until golden brown.

Air Fryer Italian Vegan Artichoke Bruschetta

Prep time: 20 minutes   Cooking Time: 10 minutes   Servings: 4

Ingredients:
- 4 slices of vegan bread
- 2 tbsp olive oil
- 200g artichoke hearts, chopped
- 1 tbsp fresh basil, chopped
- 1 clove garlic, minced
- Salt and pepper to taste

Instructions:
1. In a bowl, mix artichoke hearts, garlic, olive oil, basil, salt, and pepper.
2. Spoon the mixture onto bread slices.
3. Air fry at 180°C for 10 minutes or until crispy.

Air Fryer Thai Vegan Sweet Potato Balls

Prep time: 30 minutes | Cooking Time: 20 minutes | Servings: 4

Ingredients:
- 500g sweet potatoes, boiled and mashed
- 100g all-purpose flour
- 50g sugar
- 1 tsp black sesame seeds
- 1 tsp white sesame seeds

Instructions:
1. Mix mashed sweet potatoes, flour, and sugar until a dough forms.
2. Shape into small balls and roll in sesame seeds.
3. Air fry at 190°C for 20 minutes or until golden brown.

Air Fryer Japanese Vegan Tempura Vegetables

Prep time: 20 minutes | Cooking Time: 15 minutes | Servings: 4

Ingredients:
- Assorted vegetables (bell peppers, zucchini, sweet potato)
- 100g all-purpose flour
- 150ml cold sparkling water
- Salt to taste

Instructions:
1. Slice vegetables into bite-sized pieces.
2. Mix flour, sparkling water, and salt to form a light batter.
3. Dip vegetables in batter, ensuring they are well coated.
4. Air fry at 190°C for 15 minutes or until golden and crispy.

Air Fryer Russian Vegan Stuffed Mushrooms

Prep time: 20 minutes | Cooking Time: 20 minutes | Servings: 4

Ingredients:
- 8 large mushroom caps
- 100g breadcrumbs
- 2 cloves garlic, minced
- 2 tbsp fresh dill, chopped
- 2 tbsp olive oil
- Salt and pepper to taste

Instructions:
1. Remove stems from mushroom caps and finely chop them.
2. In a pan, heat olive oil and sauté garlic and chopped mushroom stems. Add breadcrumbs, dill, salt, and pepper. Mix well.
3. Fill each mushroom cap with the breadcrumb mixture.
4. Air fry at 190°C for 20 minutes or until mushrooms are tender.

Air Fryer African Vegan Plantain Chips

Prep time: 10 minutes | Cooking Time: 15 minutes | Servings: 4

Ingredients:
- 2 ripe plantains, thinly sliced
- 2 tbsp olive oil
- Salt and chilli powder to taste

Instructions:
1. Toss plantain slices with olive oil, salt, and chilli powder.

2. Spread the slices in a single layer on the air fryer tray.
3. Air fry at 190°C for 15 minutes or until crispy.

Air Fryer Mexican Vegan Elote Bites

Prep time: 15 minutes   Cooking Time: 20 minutes   Servings: 4

Ingredients:
- 2 ears of corn, kernels removed
- 1 tbsp lime juice
- 2 tbsp vegan mayonnaise
- 2 tbsp fresh cilantro, chopped
- 1 tsp chilli powder
- Salt to taste

Instructions:
1. Mix corn kernels with vegan mayonnaise, chilli powder, lime juice, and cilantro. Season with salt.
2. Shape the mixture into small patties.
3. Air fry at 190°C for 20 minutes or until golden and crispy.
4. Serve with a drizzle of vegan sour cream and a sprinkle of paprika.

Air Fryer British Vegan "Fish" and Chips

Prep time: 30 minutes   Cooking Time: 25 minutes   Servings: 4

Ingredients:
- 200g firm tofu, sliced into "fish" fillets
- 150g all-purpose flour
- 2 large potatoes, sliced into chips
- 2 sheets of nori seaweed
- 200ml sparkling water
- Salt and vinegar to taste

Instructions:
1. Wrap each tofu slice with a piece of nori seaweed.
2. Create a batter using flour and sparkling water.
3. Dip each tofu piece into the batter, ensuring it's well-coated.
4. Air fry tofu and chips at 190°C for 25 minutes or until golden and crispy.
5. Serve with a sprinkle of salt and a splash of vinegar.

Air Fryer Middle Eastern Vegan Spinach Fatayer

Prep time: 40 minutes   Cooking Time: 20 minutes   Servings: 4

Ingredients:
- Vegan dough
- 2 cloves garlic, minced
- 200g fresh spinach, finely chopped
- 1 tsp sumac
- Salt to taste
- 1 onion, finely choppe
- 2 tbsp olive oil

Instructions:
1. In a pan, sauté onions and garlic in olive oil until translucent.
2. Add spinach and cook until wilted. Season with sumac and salt.
3. Roll out the dough and cut into circles.
4. Place a spoonful of the spinach mixture in the centre, then fold and seal.
5. Air fry at 190°C for 20 minutes or until golden brown.

Air Fryer Italian Vegan Stuffed Olives

Prep time: 20 minutes   Cooking Time: 10 minutes   Servings: 4

Ingredients:
- 20 large green olives, pitted
- 2 tbsp olive oil
- 100g vegan cheese, grated
- 1 tsp dried oregano
- 50g breadcrumbs

Instructions:
1. Stuff each olive with a pinch of vegan cheese.
2. Mix breadcrumbs with oregano.
3. Roll the stuffed olives in olive oil, then coat with the breadcrumb mixture.
4. Air fry at 190°C for 10 minutes or until golden brown.

Bacon-Wrapped Jalapeño Poppers

Prep time: 5 minutes   Cook Time: 15 minutes   Servings: 2

Ingredients:
- 12 jalapeño peppers
- 230g cream cheese, softened
- 12 slices bacon, cut in half

Instructions:
1. Preheat your Ninja Dual Zone Air Fryer to 190°C.
2. Cut each jalapeño pepper in half lengthwise and remove the seeds.
3. Fill each jalapeño half with cream cheese, using about 1 tablespoon per pepper.
4. Wrap each filled jalapeño half with a slice of bacon, securing with a toothpick if needed.
5. Place the bacon-wrapped jalapeño poppers in the air fryer drawer.
6. Set the Zone 1 in your Ninja Dual Zone Air Fryer to "AIR FRY" and cook in the air fryer for 12-15 minutes or until the bacon is crispy.

Fried Pickles

Prep time: 15 minutes   Cook time: 8 minutes   Serves: 4

Ingredients:
- 200g pickles, sliced into thin rounds
- 2 large eggs, beaten
- 1/2 tsp paprika
- Salt and black pepper, to taste
- 100g all-purpose flour
- 100g breadcrumbs
- 1/2 tsp garlic powder
- Vegetable oil, for frying

Instructions:
1. Preheat the Ninja Dual Zone Air Fryer to 200°C on zone 1 for 5 minutes.
2. In a shallow dish, combine the all-purpose flour, paprika, garlic powder, salt, and black pepper.
3. Dip each pickle slice into the flour mixture, shaking off any excess.
4. Dip the floured pickle slice into the beaten eggs, then roll it in breadcrumbs to coat thoroughly.
5. Place the coated pickles in zone 1 of the air fryer, leaving space between them.
6. Cook the fried pickles at 200°C for 6-8 minutes, or until they are golden brown and crispy.
7. Once cooked, remove the fried pickles from the air fryer and let them cool for a minute.

Chapter 8 Soups and Stews

Air Fryer Tomato Basil Soup

Prep time: 10 minutes　　　Cooking Time: 25 minutes　　　Servings: 4

Ingredients:
- 500g ripe tomatoes, halved
- 500ml vegetable broth
- Salt and pepper to taste
- 1 onion, quartered
- 50g fresh basil leaves
- 3 cloves garlic
- 2 tbsp olive oil

Instructions:
1. Toss tomatoes, onion, and garlic in olive oil. Air fry at 200°C for 15 minutes until slightly charred.
2. Blend the roasted vegetables with vegetable broth and basil until smooth.
3. Heat in a pot until simmering. Season with salt and pepper.

Air Fryer Moroccan Lentil Stew

Prep time: 15 minutes　　　Cooking Time: 30 minutes　　　Servings: 4

Ingredients:
- 200g green lentils
- 2 cloves garlic, minced
- 1 tsp ground coriander
- Salt and pepper to taste
- 1 onion, chopped
- 500ml vegetable broth
- 1 tsp paprika
- 2 carrots, diced
- 2 tsp ground cumin
- 2 tbsp olive oil

Instructions:
1. Toss onion, carrots, and garlic in olive oil. Air fry at 190°C for 10 minutes.
2. Combine roasted vegetables, lentils, spices, and vegetable broth in a pot. Simmer for 20 minutes or until lentils are tender.
3. Season with salt and pepper.

Air Fryer Creamy Mushroom Soup

Prep time: 10 minutes　　　Cooking Time: 25 minutes　　　Servings: 4

Ingredients:
- 300g mixed mushrooms, sliced
- 2 cloves garlic, minced
- 100ml heavy cream
- Salt and pepper to taste
- 1 onion, chopped
- 500ml vegetable broth
- 2 tbsp olive oil

Instructions:
1. Toss mushrooms, onion, and garlic in olive oil. Air fry at 190°C for 15 minutes.
2. Blend half the roasted mushrooms with vegetable broth until smooth. Combine with the rest of the mushrooms.
3. Heat in a pot, add heavy cream, and season with salt and pepper.

Air Fryer Spicy Thai Coconut Soup (Tom Kha Gai)

Prep time: 15 minutes   Cooking Time: 20 minutes   Servings: 4

Ingredients:
- 200g chicken breast, sliced
- 1 lemongrass stalk, smashed
- 500ml coconut milk
- 1 tbsp lime juice
- 2 tbsp olive oil
- 200g shiitake mushrooms, sliced
- 3 kaffir lime leaves
- 2 tbsp fish sauce
- 2 red chillies, sliced

Instructions:
1. Toss chicken and mushrooms in olive oil. Air fry at 190°C for 10 minutes.
2. In a pot, combine coconut milk, lemongrass, lime leaves, and air-fried chicken and mushrooms. Simmer for 10 minutes.
3. Add fish sauce, lime juice, and chillies. Adjust seasoning to taste.

Air Fryer Hungarian Beef Goulash

Prep time: 20 minutes   Cooking Time: 40 minutes   Servings: 4

Ingredients:
- 300g beef cubes
- 2 cloves garlic, minced
- 2 tbsp olive oil
- 2 bell peppers, chopped
- 500ml beef broth
- Salt and pepper to taste
- 1 onion, chopped
- 3 tbsp paprika

Instructions:
1. Toss beef, bell peppers, onion, and garlic in olive oil. Air fry at 200°C for 15 minutes.
2. In a pot, combine air-fried Ingredients, beef broth, and paprika. Simmer for 25 minutes or until the beef is tender.
3. Season with salt and pepper.

Air Fryer Spanish Gazpacho

Prep time: 15 minutes   Cooking Time: 10 minutes   Servings: 4

Ingredients:
- 500g ripe tomatoes, chopped
- 1 onion, chopped
- 2 tbsp red wine vinegar
- 1 cucumber, chopped
- 2 cloves garlic
- Salt and pepper to taste
- 1 bell pepper, chopped
- 3 tbsp olive oil

Instructions:
1. Toss bell pepper, onion, and garlic in 1 tbsp of olive oil. Air fry at 190°C for 10 minutes.
2. Blend air-fried vegetables with tomatoes, cucumber, remaining olive oil, and red wine vinegar until smooth.
3. Chill in the refrigerator for at least 2 hours. Season with salt and pepper before serving.

Air Fryer Russian Borscht

Prep time: 20 minutes   Cooking Time: 30 minutes   Servings: 4

Ingredients:
- 300g beetroot, peeled and chopped
- 1 onion, chopped
- 100ml sour cream
- Salt and pepper to taste
- 2 cloves garlic, minced
- 2 tbsp dill, chopped
- 1 carrot, chopped
- 500ml vegetable broth
- 2 tbsp olive oil

Instructions:
1. Toss beetroot, carrot, onion, and garlic in olive oil. Air fry at 190°C for 15 minutes.
2. In a pot, combine air-fried vegetables and vegetable broth. Simmer for 15 minutes or until vegetables are tender.
3. Serve with a dollop of sour cream and a sprinkle of dill.

Air Fryer Japanese Miso Soup with Tofu

Prep time: 10 minutes Cooking Time: 10 minutes Servings: 4

Ingredients:
- 100g tofu, cubed
- 2 green onions, sliced
- 4 tbsp miso paste
- 2 tbsp olive oil
- 500ml water
- 1 sheet nori (seaweed), torn into pieces

Instructions:
1. Toss tofu cubes in olive oil. Air fry at 180°C for 10 minutes or until slightly crispy.
2. In a pot, dissolve miso paste in water. Add air-fried tofu, green onions, and nori. Heat until just simmering.

Air Fryer French Onion Soup

Prep time: 15 minutes Cooking Time: 35 minutes Servings: 4

Ingredients:
- 4 large onions, thinly sliced
- 100g grated Gruyère cheese
- 3 tbsp olive oil
- Salt and pepper to taste
- 750ml beef broth
- 4 slices of baguette
- 1 tsp sugar

Instructions:
1. Toss onions in olive oil and sugar. Air fry at 190°C for 25 minutes or until caramelised.
2. In a pot, combine caramelised onions and beef broth. Simmer for 10 minutes.
3. Serve soup in bowls, topped with a slice of baguette and sprinkled with Gruyère cheese.

Air Fryer Brazilian Black Bean Soup (Feijoada)

Prep time: 20 minutes Cooking Time: 40 minutes Servings: 4

Ingredients:
- 400g black beans, soaked overnight
- 1 onion, chopped
- 750ml water
- Salt and pepper to taste
- 200g sausage, sliced
- 2 cloves garlic, minced
- 2 tbsp olive oil

Instructions:
1. Toss sausage slices in olive oil. Air fry at 190°C for 10 minutes or until crispy.
2. In a pot, sauté onions and garlic until translucent. Add beans, water, and air-fried sausage. Simmer for 30 minutes or until the beans are tender.
3. Season with salt and pepper.

Air Fryer Irish Potato Leek Soup

Prep time: 15 minutes   Cooking Time: 30 minutes   Servings: 4

Ingredients:
- 500g potatoes, peeled and diced
- 3 cloves garlic, minced
- 100ml heavy cream
- Salt and pepper to taste
- 2 leeks, cleaned and sliced
- 750ml vegetable broth
- 2 tbsp olive oil

Instructions:
1. Toss potatoes and leeks in olive oil. Air fry at 190°C for 20 minutes.
2. In a pot, combine air-fried potatoes and leeks, garlic, and vegetable broth. Simmer for 10 minutes.
3. Blend the soup to desired consistency, then stir in heavy cream. Season with salt and pepper.

Air Fryer Mexican Tortilla Soup

Prep time: 20 minutes   Cooking Time: 25 minutes   Servings: 4

Ingredients:
- 4 corn tortillas, cut into strips
- 2 cloves garlic, minced
- 200g shredded chicken
- 1 tsp cumin
- 2 tomatoes, chopped
- 1 jalapeno, chopped
- 1 avocado, sliced
- Salt and pepper to taste
- 1 onion, chopped
- 750ml chicken broth
- 2 tbsp olive oil
- Fresh cilantro for garnish

Instructions:
1. Toss tortilla strips in 1 tbsp of olive oil. Air fry at 190°C for 5 minutes or until crispy.
2. In a pot, sauté onions, garlic, and jalapeno in the remaining olive oil until translucent. Add tomatoes, cumin, and chicken broth. Simmer for 15 minutes.
3. Add shredded chicken to the soup and cook for an additional 5 minutes.
4. Serve soup topped with crispy tortilla strips, avocado slices, and fresh cilantro.

Air Fryer Italian Minestrone Soup

Prep time: 20 minutes   Cooking Time: 30 minutes   Servings: 4

Ingredients:
- 100g pasta shells
- 1 onion, chopped
- 750ml vegetable broth
- 1 tsp dried basil
- Grated Parmesan cheese for garnish
- 2 carrots, diced
- 2 cloves garlic, minced
- 100g spinach
- Salt and pepper to taste
- 1 zucchini, diced
- 400g canned tomatoes
- 2 tbsp olive oil

Instructions:
1. Toss carrots, zucchini, and onion in olive oil. Air fry at 190°C for 15 minutes.
2. In a pot, sauté garlic in a bit of olive oil until fragrant. Add canned tomatoes, vegetable broth, dried basil, and air-fried vegetables. Simmer for 15 minutes.
3. Add pasta shells to the soup and cook until al dente. Stir in spinach until wilted.
4. Season with salt and pepper. Serve topped with grated Parmesan cheese.

Air Fryer African Peanut Stew

Cooking Time: 35 minutes Servings: 4

Ingredients:
- 200g chicken thighs, diced
- 2 cloves garlic, minced
- 150g creamy peanut butter
- 1 tsp paprika
- Chopped peanuts for garnish
- 1 sweet potato, diced
- 400ml canned tomatoes
- 2 tbsp olive oil
- Salt and pepper to taste
- 1 onion, chopped
- 500ml chicken broth
- 1 tsp ground cumin

Instructions:
1. Toss chicken, sweet potato, and onion in olive oil. Air fry at 190°C for 20 minutes.
2. In a pot, sauté garlic in olive oil until fragrant. Add canned tomatoes, chicken broth, peanut butter, cumin, paprika, and air-fried Ingredients. Simmer for 15 minutes.
3. Season with salt and pepper. Serve topped with chopped peanuts.

Air Fryer Thai Coconut Soup (Tom Kha Gai)

Prep time: 20 minutes Cooking Time: 30 minutes Servings: 4

Ingredients:
- 200g chicken breast, sliced
- 250ml chicken broth
- 4 kaffir lime leaves
- 2 tbsp fish sauce
- 1 tbsp olive oil
- 100g mushrooms, sliced
- Fresh coriander for garnish
- 400ml coconut milk
- 3 stalks lemongrass, smashed
- 4 slices galangal
- 2 tsp sugar
- 2 red chilies, sliced
- Juice of 1 lime

Instructions:
1. Toss chicken slices in olive oil. Air fry at 190°C for 10 minutes or until golden.
2. In a pot, combine coconut milk, chicken broth, lemongrass, lime leaves, and galangal. Bring to a simmer.
3. Add air-fried chicken, fish sauce, sugar, red chilies, and mushrooms. Cook for 20 minutes.
4. Before serving, add lime juice and garnish with fresh coriander.

Chapter 9 Snacks

Air Fryer Brazilian Coxinhas (Chicken Croquettes)

Prep time: 30 minutes | Cooking Time: 15 minutes | Servings: 6

Ingredients:
- 200g cooked and shredded chicken
- 1 onion, minced
- Salt and pepper, to taste
- 200ml chicken broth
- 2 cloves garlic, minced
- 1 egg, beaten
- 150g flour
- 50g cream cheese
- 150g breadcrumbs

Instructions:
1. Sauté onion and garlic. Mix in chicken and cream cheese.
2. In a pot, heat broth and slowly add flour, stirring until dough forms.
3. Take portions of dough, fill with chicken mix, and shape into drumsticks.
4. Dip in beaten egg, then coat with breadcrumbs.
5. Air fry at 190°C for 15 minutes or until golden.

Air Fryer Italian Arancini (Rice Balls)

Prep time: 25 minutes | Cooking Time: 12 minutes | Servings: 4

Ingredients:
- 200g cooked risotto rice
- 50g breadcrumbs
- 50g mozzarella, cubed
- 2 eggs, beaten
- 50g cooked ground meat (beef or pork)
- Salt and pepper, to taste

Instructions:
1. Mix risotto rice with ground meat. Season with salt and pepper.
2. Form balls and insert a mozzarella cube in the centre.
3. Dip in beaten egg, then coat with breadcrumbs.
4. Air fry at 180°C for 12 minutes or until golden.

Air Fryer Korean Tteokbokki (Spicy Rice Cakes)

Prep time: 20 minutes | Cooking Time: 10 minutes | Servings: 4

Ingredients:
- 200g rice cakes
- 1 tbsp soy sauce
- 1 tsp sesame seeds
- 50ml water
- 1 tbsp sugar
- 2 tbsp gochujang (Korean red chili paste)
- 2 green onions, sliced

Instructions:
1. Mix water, gochujang, soy sauce, and sugar to form a sauce.
2. Toss rice cakes in the sauce.
3. Air fry at 180°C for 10 minutes, stirring midway.
4. Garnish with green onions and sesame seeds.

Air Fryer Indian Samosas

Prep time: 40 minutes | Cooking Time: 15 minutes | Servings: 6

Ingredients:
- 200g all-purpose flour
- 1 onion, finely chopped
- 1 tsp garam masala
- 100g boiled potatoes, mashed
- 2 green chilies, minced
- Salt, to taste
- 50g green peas
- 1 tsp cumin seeds
- Water, for dough

Instructions:
1. Mix flour, a pinch of salt, and water to form a dough. Rest for 30 minutes.
2. Sauté onions, cumin seeds, and chilies. Add potatoes, peas, garam masala, and salt.
3. Roll out dough, cut circles, and fill with the potato mix. Seal edges.
4. Air fry at 180°C for 15 minutes or until golden.

Air Fryer Greek Spanakopita (Spinach Pie)

Prep time: 30 minutes Cooking Time: 12 minutes Servings: 4

Ingredients:
- 200g spinach, chopped
- 50g dill, chopped
- 50ml olive oil
- 100g feta cheese, crumbled
- Salt and pepper, to taste
- 2 eggs, beaten
- 8 sheets phyllo dough

Instructions:
1. Mix spinach, feta, eggs, dill, salt, and pepper.
2. Brush phyllo sheets with olive oil, place a portion of the mix, and fold into triangles.
3. Air fry at 180°C for 12 minutes or until crispy.

Air Fryer Moroccan Lamb Kefta Meatballs

Prep time: 20 minutes Cooking Time: 10 minutes Servings: 4

Ingredients:
- 200g ground lamb
- 2 tbsp fresh coriander, chopped
- Salt and pepper, to taste
- 2 garlic cloves, minced
- 1 tsp cumin powder
- 1 small onion, finely chopped
- 1 tsp paprika

Instructions:
1. Mix all Ingredients in a bowl.
2. Form into small meatballs.
3. Air fry at 190°C for 10 minutes or until browned and cooked through.

Air Fryer Australian Vegemite and Cheese Scrolls

Prep time: 25 minutes Cooking Time: 12 minutes Servings: 6

Ingredients:
- 250g self-raising flour
- 150ml milk
- 2 tbsp Vegemite
- 100g cheddar cheese, grated

Instructions:
1. Mix flour and milk to form a dough.
2. Roll out into a rectangle.
3. Spread Vegemite and sprinkle cheese.
4. Roll up and cut into scrolls.
5. Air fry at 180°C for 12 minutes or until golden.

Air Fryer Mexican Taquitos

Prep time: 30 minutes Cooking Time: 10 minutes Servings: 4

Ingredients:
- 200g cooked chicken, shredded
- 50g salsa
- 8 small corn tortillas
- 1 tsp chili powder
- 100g cheddar cheese, grated
- 1 tsp cumin
- Salt, to taste

Instructions:
1. Mix chicken, salsa, chili powder, cumin, and salt.
2. Place a portion of the mix on each tortilla, sprinkle cheese, and roll tightly.
3. Air fry at 190°C for 10 minutes or until crispy.

Air Fryer Thai Sweet Potato Balls

Prep time: 30 minutes　　　Cooking Time: 12 minutes　　　Servings: 4

Ingredients:
- 200g sweet potatoes, boiled and mashed
- 50g tapioca flour
- 50g sugar
- Pinch of salt

Instructions:
1. Mix mashed sweet potatoes, tapioca flour, sugar, and salt to form a dough.
2. Roll into small balls.
3. Air fry at 180°C for 12 minutes or until golden brown.

Air Fryer British Scotch Eggs

Prep time: 25 minutes　　　Cooking Time: 12 minutes　　　Servings: 4

Ingredients:
- 4 eggs, soft-boiled
- Salt and pepper, to taste
- 200g sausage meat
- 1 egg, beaten
- 1 tsp dried thyme
- 150g breadcrumbs

Instructions:
1. Mix sausage meat, thyme, salt, and pepper.
2. Encase each soft-boiled egg with the meat mixture.
3. Dip in beaten egg and coat with breadcrumbs.
4. Air fry at 190°C for 12 minutes or until browned.

Air Fryer German Pretzel Bites

Prep time: 2 hours (includes dough resting)　　　Cooking Time: 10 minutes　　　Servings: 6

Ingredients:
- 250g all-purpose flour
- 1 tbsp sugar
- Coarse sea salt, for sprinkling
- 1 tsp instant yeast
- 1 tsp salt
- 150ml warm water
- 2 tbsp baking soda

Instructions:
1. Combine flour, yeast, warm water, sugar, and salt to form a dough. Let it rest for 1. 5 hours.
2. Divide and roll into bite-sized balls.
3. Dip each ball into a baking soda-water solution.
4. Sprinkle with coarse salt.

5. Air fry at 190°C for 10 minutes or until golden.

Air Fryer Jamaican Jerk Chicken Wings

Prep time: 20 minutes + marination   Cooking Time: 15 minutes   Servings: 4

Ingredients:
- 500g chicken wings
- 1 tbsp honey
- 2 tbsp jerk seasoning
- 1 lime, juiced
- 1 tbsp soy sauce
- Salt to taste

Instructions:
1. Marinate chicken wings with jerk seasoning, soy sauce, honey, lime juice, and salt for at least 2 hours.
2. Air fry at 190°C for 15 minutes or until fully cooked and crispy.

Air Fryer Vietnamese Spring Rolls

Prep time: 30 minutes   Cooking Time: 10 minutes   Servings: 4

Ingredients:
- 8 rice paper sheets
- 50g shrimp, cooked and sliced
- 1 carrot, julienned
- 50g vermicelli noodles, cooked
- 50g lettuce, chopped
- Fresh mint and cilantro

Instructions:
1. Wet rice paper sheets briefly.
2. Layer vermicelli, shrimp, lettuce, carrot, mint, and cilantro.
3. Roll tightly, tucking in the sides.
4. Air fry at 180°C for 10 minutes or until crispy.

Air Fryer Russian Pirozhki (Stuffed Buns)

Prep time: 2 hours (includes dough rising)   Cooking Time: 12 minutes   Servings: 6

Ingredients:
- 250g all-purpose flour
- 1 tbsp sugar
- 1 onion, finely chopped
- 1 tsp instant yeast
- 1 tsp salt
- Salt and pepper, to taste
- 150ml warm milk
- 100g minced meat (beef or chicken)

Instructions:
1. Combine flour, yeast, warm milk, sugar, and salt to form a dough. Let rise for 1. 5 hours.
2. Sauté onion and meat. Season with salt and pepper.
3. Divide dough and fill with the meat mixture. Seal edges.
4. Air fry at 190°C for 12 minutes or until golden.

Air Fryer Kenyan Bhajia (Potato Fritters)

Prep time: 20 minutes   Cooking Time: 12 minutes   Servings: 4

Ingredients:
- 200g potatoes, thinly sliced
- 100g gram flour (chickpea flour)
- 1 tsp chili powder

- 1 tsp turmeric powder
- Salt to taste
- 150ml water

Instructions:
1. Mix gram flour, chili powder, turmeric, salt, and water to form a batter.
2. Dip potato slices in the batter, ensuring they're well-coated.
3. Air fry at 190°C for 12 minutes or until crispy.

Meatballs with Hot Dipping Sauce

Prep time: 10 minutes Cook time: 20 minutes Serves 5

Ingredients
- **Meatballs:**
- 500g turkey mince, 93% lean and 7% fat
- 300g pork mince
- 120g porridge oats
- 2 cloves garlic, minced
- 1 medium egg, beaten
- 1 tsp ground cumin
- 1 tsp coriander seeds
- Sea salt and ground black pepper, to taste
- 1 tbsp olive oil
- **Dipping Sauce:**
- 20ml honey
- 100ml hot sauce
- 2 tbsp butter

Instructions
1. In a mixing bowl, thoroughly combine all the Ingredients for the meatballs. Shape the mixture into equal balls.
2. Select zone 1 and pair it with "AIR FRY" at 185°C for 20 minutes. Select "MATCH" to duplicate settings across both zones. Press the "START/STOP" button.
3. At the halfway point, turn the meatballs over and reinsert the drawers to resume cooking.
4. Preheat a saucepan over medium-high heat; melt the butter and then, add hot sauce and honey.
5. Serve warm meatballs with cocktail sticks and dipping sauce on the side.

Mini Apple Pies

Serves: 4 Prep time: 20 minutes Cook time: 12 minutes

Ingredients:
- 2 apples, peeled, cored, and diced
- 50g granulated sugar
- 1/2 tsp ground cinnamon
- 1/4 tsp ground nutmeg
- 1 tbsp lemon juice
- 8 small pre-made pie crusts
- 2 tbsp unsalted butter, melted
- Icing sugar, for dusting

Instructions:
1. Preheat the Ninja Dual Zone Air Fryer to 190°C in zone 1 for 5 minutes.
2. In a bowl, combine the diced apples, granulated sugar, ground cinnamon, ground nutmeg, and lemon juice. Mix well to coat the apples with the sugar and spices.
3. Roll out the pie crusts and cut them into smaller circles to fit your silicone muffin cups.
4. Press each pie crust circle into a silicone muffin cup, forming a small pie shell.
5. Fill each pie shell with the apple mixture, dividing it evenly among the cups.
6. Brush the melted butter over the top of each mini apple pie.
7. Place the mini apple pies in zone 1 of the air fryer, leaving space between them.
8. Cook the pies at 190°C for 10-12 minutes, or until the crust is golden brown and the apples are tender.
9. Once cooked, remove the mini apple pies from the air fryer and let them cool for a minute.

Chapter 10 Chapter Desserts

Air Fryer Italian Cannoli

Prep time: 20 minutes Cooking Time: 8 minutes Servings: 6

Ingredients:
- 6 cannoli shells
- 100g powdered sugar
- Zest of 1 orange
- 250g ricotta cheese
- 50g chocolate chips

Instructions:
1. In a bowl, combine ricotta cheese, powdered sugar, chocolate chips, and orange zest.
2. Pipe the filling into cannoli shells.
3. Air fry at 160°C for 8 minutes until golden brown.

Air Fryer French Madeleines

Prep time: 15 minutes Cooking Time: 10 minutes Servings: 12

Ingredients:
- 100g all-purpose flour
- 100g melted butter
- 1 tsp vanilla extract
- 100g sugar
- 2 eggs
- Zest of 1 lemon

Instructions:
1. Beat eggs and sugar until light and fluffy. Mix in butter, vanilla, and lemon zest.
2. Fold in the flour gently.
3. Pour batter into madeleine moulds.
4. Air fry at 170°C for 10 minutes until golden.

Air Fryer Japanese Mochi

Prep time: 30 minutes (plus cooling time) Cooking Time: 12 minutes Servings: 8

Ingredients:
- 200g glutinous rice flour (mochiko)
- 240ml water
- Anko (red bean paste) for filling
- 150g sugar
- Cornstarch for dusting

Instructions:
1. Mix rice flour, sugar, and water to form a smooth batter.
2. Pour into a lined dish and steam for 20 minutes until set.
3. Once cooled, divide and fill with anko paste.
4. Shape into balls and coat with cornstarch.
5. Air fry at 150°C for 12 minutes.

Air Fryer American Brownie Bites

| Prep time: 15 minutes | Cooking Time: 10 minutes | Servings: 12 |

Ingredients:
- 100g melted chocolate
- 2 eggs
- 75g sugar
- 50g all-purpose flour
- 50g butter

Instructions:
1. Mix melted chocolate, sugar, and butter.
2. Beat in the eggs.
3. Fold in the flour.
4. Pour batter into mini muffin moulds.
5. Air fry at 180°C for 10 minutes.

Air Fryer Indian Gulab Jamun

| Prep time: 30 minutes | Cooking Time: 8 minutes | Servings: 10 |

Ingredients:
- 100g milk powder
- 1 tsp oil
- 500ml water
- 50g all-purpose flour
- 1 tsp baking soda
- 2 tsp rose water
- 50ml milk
- 250g sugar

Instructions:
1. Combine milk powder, flour, milk, oil, and baking soda to form a dough.
2. Shape into balls.
3. Air fry at 180°C for 8 minutes until golden.
4. Prepare syrup by boiling sugar, water, and rose water.
5. Soak the fried balls in the syrup for 2 hours.

Air Fryer British Scones

| Prep time: 20 minutes | Cooking Time: 12 minutes | Servings: 8 |

Ingredients:
- 225g self-raising flour
- 25g sugar
- 1 tsp baking powder
- 55g butter, softened
- 150ml milk
- Pinch of salt

Instructions:
1. Mix the flour, baking powder, and salt. Rub in the butter.
2. Stir in the sugar, then gradually add milk to get a soft dough.
3. Turn onto a floured work surface and knead briefly.
4. Cut into rounds using a cutter.
5. Air fry at 180°C for 12 minutes until risen and golden.

Air Fryer Moroccan Coconut Ghriba

| Prep time: 15 minutes | Cooking Time: 10 minutes | Servings: 12 |

Ingredients:
- 200g desiccated coconut
- 2 eggs
- 100g sugar
- 1 tsp vanilla extract

Instructions:
1. Combine all the Ingredients to form a dough.
2. Shape into small balls and flatten slightly.
3. Air fry at 170°C for 10 minutes until lightly golden.

Air Fryer Australian Lamingtons

Prep time: 30 minutes Cooking Time: 15 minutes Servings: 10

Ingredients:
- 200g self-raising flour
- 4 eggs
- 100g cocoa powder
- 200g sugar
- 100g melted butter
- 200g desiccated coconut

Instructions:
1. Whisk eggs and sugar until creamy. Fold in sifted flour and melted butter.
2. Pour into a square tin and bake for 20 minutes.
3. Once cooled, cut into squares. Dip each in cocoa powder and then coat in coconut.
4. Air fry at 160°C for 15 minutes.

Air Fryer Russian Sharlotka (Apple Cake)

Prep time: 20 minutes Cooking Time: 20 minutes Servings: 8

Ingredients:
- 3 apples, peeled and sliced
- 200g flour
- 1 tsp vanilla extract
- 200g sugar
- 3 eggs
- 1 tsp baking powder

Instructions:
1. Beat eggs and sugar until creamy. Add vanilla, then fold in sifted flour and baking powder.
2. Add apples to the batter and mix.
3. Pour into a greased cake tin.
4. Air fry at 180°C for 20 minutes.

Air Fryer Chinese Red Bean Buns

Prep time: 30 minutes (plus resting time) Cooking Time: 15 minutes Servings: 8

Ingredients:
- 300g all-purpose flour
- 1 tsp yeast
- 150ml warm water
- 200g red bean paste

Instructions:
1. Dissolve yeast in warm water. Mix with flour to form a dough.
2. Let it rest for 2 hours.

3. Divide into small balls and flatten. Fill with red bean paste and seal.
4. Air fry at 160°C for 15 minutes.

Air Fryer Filipino Turon (Banana Spring Rolls)

Prep time: 15 minutes   Cooking Time: 10 minutes   Servings: 8

Ingredients:
- 4 ripe bananas, sliced lengthwise
- 100g brown sugar
- 8 spring roll wrappers
- 1 tsp vanilla extract

Instructions:
1. Coat each banana slice in brown sugar.
2. Place a banana slice on a spring roll wrapper and roll tightly.
3. Air fry at 180°C for 10 minutes or until golden brown.

Air Fryer Dutch Poffertjes (Mini Pancakes)

Prep time: 20 minutes   Cooking Time: 5 minutes   Servings: 30 mini pancakes

Ingredients:
- 125g all-purpose flour
- 1 egg
- 50g melted butter
- 125ml milk
- 1 tsp baking powder
- Powdered sugar for serving

Instructions:
1. Whisk together flour, milk, egg, and baking powder until smooth.
2. Pour small amounts of batter into mini muffin molds.
3. Air fry at 170°C for 5 minutes until puffy and golden.
4. Serve with a sprinkle of powdered sugar and a dab of butter.

Air Fryer Greek Loukoumades (Honey Balls)

Prep time: 20 minutes (plus resting)   Cooking Time: 10 minutes   Servings: 20 balls

Ingredients:
- 250g all-purpose flour
- 2 tsp yeast
- 1 tsp cinnamon
- 200ml warm water
- 50g honey

Instructions:
1. Dissolve yeast in warm water. Mix with flour to form a batter.
2. Let it rest for an hour.
3. Drop spoonfuls of batter into the air fryer.
4. Air fry at 180°C for 10 minutes until golden.
5. Drizzle with honey and sprinkle with cinnamon.

Air Fryer Brazilian Brigadeiros (Chocolate Truffles)

Prep time: 15 minutes   Cooking Time: 10 minutes   Servings: 20 truffles

Ingredients:
- 395g sweetened condensed milk
- 30g butter
- 30g cocoa powder
- Chocolate sprinkles for rolling

Instructions:
1. Mix condensed milk, cocoa powder, and butter in a pan. Cook until thickened.
2. Let it cool and shape into small balls.
3. Air fry at 160°C for 10 minutes.
4. Roll in chocolate sprinkles while still warm.

Air Fryer South African Malva Pudding

Prep time: 25 minutes   Cooking Time: 20 minutes   Servings: 8

Ingredients:
- 200g sugar
- 1 tbsp apricot jam
- 2 tsp baking soda
- 2 tbsp vinegar
- 2 eggs
- 220g all-purpose flour
- 250ml warm milk
- 50g melted butter

Instructions:
1. Beat sugar and eggs until creamy. Mix in jam.
2. Add flour and baking soda. Mix well.
3. Stir in milk, vinegar, and butter.
4. Pour into a baking dish.
5. Air fry at 170°C for 20 minutes until set and golden.

Chocolate Lava Cakes

Serves: 4   Prep time: 10 minutes   Cook time: 12 minutes

Ingredients:
- 100g dark chocolate
- 2 large eggs
- 30g all-purpose flour
- Cooking spray or extra butter, for greasing
- Icing sugar, for dusting
- 100g unsalted butter
- 60g granulated sugar
- Pinch of salt
- Fresh berries, for garnish (optional)

Instructions:
1. Preheat the Ninja Dual Zone Air Fryer to 180°C on zone 1 for 5 minutes.
2. In a microwave-safe bowl, melt the dark chocolate and butter together in short bursts, stirring in between, until smooth. Let it cool slightly.
3. In a separate bowl, whisk the eggs and granulated sugar together until well combined.
4. Gradually add the melted chocolate mixture to the egg mixture, whisking constantly.
5. Sift in the flour and salt, and gently fold until just combined.
6. Grease 4 ramekins or silicone muffin cups with cooking spray or butter.
7. Divide the batter evenly among the greased ramekins or cups.
8. Place the ramekins or cups in zone 1 of the air fryer and cook at 180°C for 12 minutes or until the edges are set but the centres are still slightly gooey.

9. Once cooked, remove the lava cakes from the air fryer and let them cool for a minute.
10. Carefully invert the cakes onto serving plates and dust with icing sugar. Garnish with fresh berries if desired. Serve immediately and enjoy the rich and decadent chocolate lava cakes.

Bread Pudding with Caramel Sauce

Serves: 4　　　　Prep time: 15 minutes　　　　Cook time: 30 minutes

Ingredients:
- 4 slices day-old bread, cubed
- 2 large eggs
- 1 tsp vanilla extract
- Pinch of salt
- 300ml whole milk
- 80g granulated sugar
- 1/2 tsp ground cinnamon
- Caramel sauce, for serving

Instructions:
1. Preheat the Ninja Dual Zone Air Fryer to 180°C on zone 1 for 5 minutes.
2. In a bowl, combine the bread cubes and milk, allowing the bread to soak for a few minutes.
3. In another bowl, whisk together the eggs, granulated sugar, vanilla extract, ground cinnamon, and salt.
4. Pour the egg mixture over the soaked bread cubes, stirring gently to combine.
5. Grease a baking dish or silicone baking mould.
6. Transfer the bread mixture to the greased dish or mould, spreading it evenly.
7. Place the dish or mould in zone 1 of the air fryer and cook at 180°C for 30 minutes or until the top is golden brown and the pudding is set.
8. Once cooked, remove the bread pudding from the air fryer and let it cool for a few minutes.
9. Serve the bread pudding warm, drizzled with caramel sauce. Enjoy the comforting and indulgent dessert!

Printed in Great Britain
by Amazon